Additional Praise for
Practical Psychoanalysis for Therapists and Patients

"A lot had been learned about disorders of mind before we came along: to be unaware of that legacy is to be uneducated; to be awestruck by it is to diminish one's capacity to add something new – to the loss, incidentally, of those who will come after. Without destruction, no creation. Renik grew up intellectually within the burgeoning psychoanalytic culture of the last century. He knows it well, could thread his way through its labyrinth in the dark, but has not allowed its famously close embrace to impede the movements of his own thought. He has elbowed his way free, is become a new broom in the littered corridors of psychoanalysis. Nothing useful is swept away, but nothing is left standing simply because it has been there a long time and has secured honor. Shrines are passed without a glance. Received wisdom is received without reverence, and, if useless, discarded without ceremony. No tears are shed. From the first page we know ourselves to be in a workshop, not a temple. His matter-of-factness is breathtaking: what's useful is what's important, what's not need not detain us. Cloistered space permitting of but cramped thought is become open space inviting innovation. True believers are to be warned: they may never be the same again."

– **Allen Wheelis**, author of *How People Change* and *The Way We Are*

"Renik is an outstanding clinician and theorist who has redefined the two-person therapeutic perspective. His 'one-of-a-kind' book presents clinical examples of the diversity of patient–analyst interactions, providing dazzling descriptions of clinical cases, each of which depicts turning points in the therapy. Each case demonstrates how the analyst's flexibility and intuition are key to outcome. Renik tellingly remarks that too many analysts have privileged insight over outcome. He demonstrates how 'therapeutic efficacy' must be correlated with symptom relief and how on occasion the analyst must help the patient become conscious of thoughts never previously accessed, some of which had not previously existed. His book is original, therapeutically enlightening, and will, I believe, broaden the perspective of its readers."

– **Ethel Spector Person, M.D.**, Training and Supervising Analyst, Columbia University Psychoanalytic Center for Training and Research, Coeditor of *The APPI Textbook of Psychoanalysis*

PRACTICAL PSYCHOANALYSIS
FOR THERAPISTS AND PATIENTS

OWEN RENIK

OTHER
Other Press
New York

Copyright © 2006 Owen Renik

Production Editor: Robert D. Hack

This book was set in Berkeley by Alpha Graphics of Pittsfield, New Hampshire.
ISBN-13: 978-1-59051-237-1

10 9 8 7 6 5 4 3

Library of Congress Cataloging-in-Publication Data

Renik, Owen.
    Practical psychoanalysis for therapists and patients / by Owen Renik.
        p. cm.
    ISBN 1-59051-237-5
1. Psychoanalysis. 2. Mental illness–Treatment. I. Title.
    RC504.R46 2006
    616.89'17–dc22   2005030273

Contents

Practical Psychoanalysis

By now, the term *practical psychoanalysis* has become an oxymoron. The way psychoanalytic treatment is generally conducted, it is extremely *impractical*: it doesn't serve the needs of the vast majority of potential patients. Understandably, people who seek the help of mental health caregivers want a therapy that will provide maximum relief from emotional distress as quickly as possible. Most clinical psychoanalysts offer instead a lengthy journey of self-discovery during which too much concern with symptom relief is considered counterproductive. "Self-awareness" is the main goal; symptom relief is of secondary importance and is expected to arrive, if at all, only after a while.

No surprise, then, that psychoanalysis has come to be regarded by the public at large as an esoteric practice that promotes a self-involved escape from real life, rather than a treatment method that helps the patient live real life more happily. No surprise, either, that all over the world fewer and fewer patients seek psychoanalytic treatment, and that those who do are for the most part people who want to become psychoanalysts themselves or fellow travelers who have an intellectual interest in the field. Clinical psychoanalysis has become, deservedly, the stuff of *New Yorker* cartoons.

This unfortunate state of affairs is ironic, considering that psychoanalysis got its start on the basis of its therapeutic efficacy. In the course of their researches, Breuer and Freud stumbled upon a method for relieving notoriously difficult-to-treat hysterical symptoms. Though Freud was a fascinating and imaginative writer who developed far-reaching ideas about culture and society, as well as about individual psychology, the world originally paid attention to him because of the extraordinary cures he and Breuer achieved—and achieved very rapidly, too, in contrast to the expectations of contemporary psychoanalysts.

Over the years, psychoanalysis drifted away from its original orientation toward symptom relief as the desired outcome of treatment and became increasingly preoccupied with a special, specifically psychoanalytic goal: the achievement of "insight" for its own sake. In the process, psychoanalysts not only made themselves irrelevant to most people's needs, but, as many critics have pointed out, also compromised clinical psychoanalysis as a scientific investigative tool. How can the validity of insight be assessed? Insights reached by analyst and patient together about the latter's psychology are inevitably influenced by the former's theory. Therefore, unless insights are validated by correlation with symptom relief (an outcome criterion that is not theory-driven), a closed system is set up in which successful clinical analysis consists of analyst and patient discovering what the analyst assumed a priori to exist. Impractical psychoanalysis is also unscientific psychoanalysis.

Clinical psychoanalysis has become impractical, but it does not have to be impractical. In order to offer patients practical psychoanalysis, however, clinicians cannot conduct treatment on the basis of received wisdom. To begin with, psychoanalysts cannot assume the virtue of any particular set of procedures—use of the couch, frequency of sessions, even the method of free association. These are techniques, and in the progressive development of any scientifically based clinical practice, techniques will alter, even alter dramatically, as empirical evidence accumulates; some prove valuable and are retained, others are discarded. Only two hundred years ago, for example, the best available medical science indicated that bleeding the patient through use of leeches or by venicotomy was part of the responsible standard of care for most illnesses. Almost every patient who consulted a physician was bled. We now know that this technique, which was practiced as state of the art by the best physicians for centuries, was useless in almost all cases and dangerously detrimental in many.

Similarly, we have every reason to expect that the techniques of a scientifically based clinical psychoanalysis will alter over time. Therefore, it makes no sense to define clinical psychoanalysis as a particular set of techniques. Nor does it make sense to define clinical psychoanalysis as a particular set of theories, for these, too, will alter as science progresses. Even the most fundamental psychoanalytic concepts and principles should be critically reviewed at every turn, and we can anticipate that most will eventually be found obsolete. That's what happens in science. Practical psychoanalysis means remaining open-minded with regard to theory, holding nothing as axiomatic; and it means retaining an experimental approach to technique—that is, searching for whatever way of working together with a given patient seems to make progress toward the desired goals of treatment.

If practical psychoanalysis cannot be defined in terms of any particular theory or technique, how can it be defined? The sensible way to define practical psychoanalysis is in terms of its area of study and its objectives. Sciences are usually defined in terms of their subject areas and applied sciences in terms of their objectives (e.g., chemistry is the study of compounds, and pharmaceutics is the creation of useful drugs by applying chemical knowledge). Psychoanalysis is a scientific study of the mind, and clinical psychoanalysis is an application of psychoanalytic science to therapy. Practical clinical psychoanalysis is a treatment that aims to help the patient feel less distress and more satisfaction in daily life through improved understanding of how his or her mind works. Another way to put this is to say that in a successful practical analysis the patient is able to revise various aspects of the way he or she constructs reality, with the result that the patient feels better.

We might even take a traditional view, following Freud, and add that practical analysis brings the unconscious into consciousness. However, if we want to continue to use that conception, we must be prepared to update our definition of "the unconscious." It was Freud's idea that clinical psychoanalysis brings into conscious awareness certain thoughts that are available to consciousness but remain unconscious because the patient is motivated not to be aware of them— what Freud termed *repressed* thoughts or the *dynamic unconscious*. And it is true that successful practical analysis usually does, to a certain extent, involve the patient identifying ideas, feelings, and memories that he or she has been holding out of conscious awareness for one reason or another. But it is also true that a very significant part of what happens in practical analysis consists of the patient becoming conscious of thoughts that have never been repressed, thoughts that the patient simply never had the opportunity to think before. These thoughts arise from novel perspectives provided by the analyst— explicitly or implicitly, intentionally or unintentionally—in the course of an intimate, mutually engaged exploration with the patient of his or her difficulties.

In every professional community, there are some psychoanalysts who treat patients practically. These clinicians help their patients achieve therapeutic benefits as rapidly as possible. The patients feel better, the quality of their lives improves, and their friends and families can see it. For that reason, practical psychoanalysts, contrary to the general trend, have more referrals than they can handle—and their practices are filled with patients who are neither analysts in training, nor hapless souls who are encouraged to remain for many years in treatments that produce no significant symptom relief.

Unfortunately, practical psychoanalysts tend not to publicize what they do with patients; instead, they quietly set many traditional psychoanalytic theories and techniques aside and go about doing what works. Good for practical psychoanalysts and for their patients! But not good for the field. There are many clinicians who would like to learn more about how to conduct a practical psychoanalytic treatment, and many patients who would like to know how to recognize one. This book is addressed to readers in both categories.

In the chapters that follow, I will discuss what I have found to be basic principles of practical psychoanalytic treatment. I will use a casebook format, presenting concepts via illustrative clinical examples. I do that for two reasons: first, because I find that abstract formulations about psychoanalytic theory and technique, by themselves, are difficult to understand, let alone apply on the line in work with patients; and second, because my recommendations are not based upon findings from systematic, controlled empirical research (nobody's recommendations are, in psychoanalysis, since adequate research methods have not yet been developed) and I want to share with readers, as best I can, the clinical experiences that have led me to reach my conclusions.

This is not intended as a scholarly volume. I haven't presented a survey of the literature, noting whose ideas have been the same or similar to mine and whose have been different. No background in psychoanalysis is required to understand what I have written. When I speak of an "analyst," I do not refer to someone who has attended an official psychoanalytic training program; I only mean a psychoanalytically informed psychotherapist—and since most of Freud's important ideas have long since percolated into the cultural surround, any contemporary psychotherapist who is at all eclectic in his or her orientation will inevitably be psychoanalytically informed. My aim is to discuss in a down-to-earth way what, in my experience, can be useful for both analyst and patient to keep in mind when collaborating in an effort to help the latter feel better; and I think the best way for me to do that is to offer a collection of anecdotes, together with my thoughts about them.

2

Symptoms and Symptom Relief

You can't treat a patient successfully without knowing what it is you're attempting to treat the patient for, and it's impossible to judge the progress of a treatment unless you know what the desired outcome of the treatment is supposed to be. Therefore, the crucial first step in doing effective clinical psychoanalytic work is to reach an understanding with the patient concerning what his or her symptoms are and what symptom relief would consist of.

By *symptom* I mean something about himself or herself that the patient needs to change because it is causing distress. It is the *patient* who decides what his or her symptoms are. This point cannot be overemphasized. Certainly, the process of identifying symptoms is a collaboration between patient and analyst, to which the analyst can make important contributions; but it is the patient who must have the final word, because clinical analysis doesn't work when a patient is being treated for something the patient doesn't regard as a problem—even if the analyst is convinced that it is a problem. Impasses in analysis often arise because an analyst is attempting to treat a patient for what the *analyst* thinks the patient's symptoms are, without having carefully explored the *patient's* view of what his or her symptoms are. Then, analyst and patient mistakenly assume that they are pursuing a shared objective, while in fact they have quite different ideas about symptoms and symptom relief. They work at cross purposes for some time until, eventually, the misalliance makes itself felt; and even when it does, they may not realize that a fundamental lack of consensus about the goals of treatment is responsible for their problem. The old light bulb joke says it well: How many psychoanalysts does it take to change a light bulb? Only one, but the light bulb has to want to change!

It is by no means necessary that a patient arrive with a clear idea of what his or her symptoms are in order to be treated. Very often a patient seeks help without any definite notions at all about how he or she needs to change. The patient only knows that he or she feels bad and wants to feel better. When this is the case, the first order of business is to achieve some clarity and consensus about what the patient's symptoms are and what symptom relief would mean. That task is often not easy to accomplish. Sometimes, the work needed, in itself, brings significant therapeutic benefit.

For example, some patients admit willingly that they need help, but when they describe what they need help with, their problems always turn out to be externally caused—by unsympathetic spouses, abusive coworkers, physical illnesses, or other circumstances outside their control; they see nothing about themselves that is responsible for their distress. Or, the exact opposite can be the case. Some patients are desperate to find pathological character traits in themselves that they can work on in analysis, because they want to avoid at all costs acknowledging that their distress arises from external circumstances—abusive partners who won't change, children in trouble whose disturbances they want to minimize, or other facts of life that they're reluctant to face. When a patient whose presenting complaints are based on externalization or on denial is eventually able to become clear about what his or her symptoms are, the recognition, in itself, can represent a significant achievement that brings with it considerable therapeutic benefit.

It sometimes happens that a patient is uncertain about what he or she wants to work on, and sorting out that uncertainty turns out to be all that was needed. Here is an example.

RALPH

One evening, I ran into a friend of mine at a party. The successful CEO of a large company, he was extremely skeptical about psychotherapy; so it was with a kind of grudging amusement that he said he had a story to tell me that he thought I would enjoy hearing. He had just had the pleasure of hiring for a very well-paid position a man named Ralph, whom he had known fairly well at one time, but had not seen for ten years. My friend was astonished at how Ralph had changed. Ten years ago, Ralph would never have been able to handle significant managerial responsibility. He had always been bright, but terribly depressed and ineffective. His personal life was a mess—he seemed henpecked and miserable. But now, Ralph was obviously on top of things in a very nice way. No more wishy-washiness: he was straightforward and clear. Whereas Ralph used to be self-effacing to an infuriating degree, and would endlessly qualify everything he said, he now came across as appropriately thoughtful and modest, but confident. As they caught one another up on their personal lives, my friend noted that Ralph spoke about his wife with unmistakable pleasure and affection.

So impressed was my friend with this apparent transformation that he was moved to comment on it to Ralph and to ask how it had come about. "I had a very good psychotherapy," was the answer. "I found a shrink who helped me figure out the things I needed to know about myself." Thinking that he might like to refer somebody some time to a therapist who actually helped people, my friend asked the shrink's name and was surprised to learn that Ralph had been in treatment with me. I was quite gratified by this coincidental report, of course. But what particularly interested me about it was something that Ralph had not mentioned: the very helpful psychotherapy with me that Ralph described to my friend had consisted of only one visit!

I remembered the session very well. When he had come to see me, Ralph had seemed very much as my friend described him having been years ago—troubled and tentative. Ralph talked about his general malaise, his problems at work, his marital difficulties, his fear that he was an inadequate father to his two children, and a host of related worries. He told me a bit about his background, hesitantly sketching out what I thought were probably some very shrewd insights about his mixed feelings toward a loving but somewhat dictatorial father, his conflicted identification with a quietly competent mother, and his anxieties about a younger sister who adored him.

After a time, I asked Ralph what he wanted to accomplish in therapy. He thought a moment, then answered in a way I could not possibly have foreseen. He said that what he would really like to do was to feel able to devote a year to studying guitar. Apparently, Ralph was quite a talented guitarist and passionate about the instrument. He could practice for hours without noticing the time go by. He played jazz and was good enough to sit in at clubs on open-mike nights; but he had never had any formal training, and he knew that his level of playing would improve enormously if he could spend a year consolidating his skills through study at a conservatory. He was pretty sure he could get into a good one.

Ralph did not know where this would lead; certainly, he did not expect to make a living as a professional musician, but he knew he wanted to take his guitar playing further. At the same time, he knew that to do so would mean earning no money for a while. His wife's small salary would not begin to support the family. They would have to use up their savings, and there was a very real possibility that Ralph would be unable to find another executive position when he reentered the marketplace. Ralph felt himself on the horns of an insoluble dilemma: he did not want to put his wife and children at such risk, despite their assurances that they would support him if he needed to drop out for a year; on the other hand, he remained preoccupied, distracted, and upset because nothing in his life seemed worthwhile if he could not pursue his dream.

Listening to all this, I had the impression that Ralph was not really describing a choice he was trying to make. It was more that he was describing his reluctance to act on a choice that he had already made. It seemed clear that he felt he could not be happy without studying the guitar, and that he could not study the guitar without asking his wife and children to endure a certain amount of sacrifice and risk. I conveyed this impression to Ralph, and he agreed. I asked him if he felt he had the right to do what he wanted to do. He thought quite a while before replying, and finally said that he was not sure. Probably, he did; but, in any case, he was making himself and everyone else so miserable by not doing what he wanted, that, practically speaking, there really was no good alternative. Still, he felt unable to act.

I said that there were certainly a great many relevant matters we could explore—how Ralph seemed to be looking for permission from me or some other authority; particular problems he had in balancing self-interest against a sense of responsibility toward loved ones; the special meaning that artistic creativity as opposed to business held for him; and so forth. If issues of this sort were making things more difficult than they needed to be, it would be very useful for us to investigate them together; but it was also important to keep in mind that no amount of self-awareness was going to change the circumstances with which Ralph had to deal, or the need for him to act, one way or the other, and to take responsibility for his actions. It might simply come down to a question of Ralph's having to accept that he had to do what he thought best under the circumstances—one way or the other—and live with the consequences, not all of which would be agreeable.

As I laid out the way I saw the state of affairs, Ralph kept nodding thoughtfully in agreement. Our time was about up, so I suggested that we arrange another appointment to continue to reflect and decide how Ralph might want to proceed. He agreed. The next day, however, Ralph called to say that I had given him a great deal to think about and that for the moment he felt he did not need to chat further. He would certainly give me a call when and if he did. He thanked me warmly and said that he would like to stay in touch, in any case. I asked him to please keep me posted.

A month or so later, Ralph left me a message that he had decided to take the plunge, to study guitar, and that he thought things were going to work out. For a few years, I received occasional notes telling me that he was doing well. Eventually, I learned that he was back at work and enjoying keeping up on guitar. After a while, I stopped hearing from Ralph, so that my friend's anecdote was a very welcome update.

One way to think about Ralph's single session treatment would be to say that he found out that he didn't have any symptoms. Our brief exploration of his desires and conflicts helped him see that there was nothing he could change about himself that would alter his dilemma. He simply had to make a decision and act on it, difficult as that was. Another way to think about Ralph's treatment would be to say that he got clearer about what his symptoms were: his reluctance to acknowledge that he had to make a decision and act upon it, and his unrealistic hope that he could somehow change the terms of the conflict he was facing.

I think an argument could be made for either view, and I'm not sure it matters which we choose. The important point is that it was my asking Ralph what he wanted to get out of treatment—my inquiry into what Ralph thought his symptoms were and what kind of symptom relief he was after—that produced the positive therapeutic result. It set in motion a process of self-investigation (which Ralph conducted largely on his own, not with me) that concluded very happily for him. It hardly matters whether we say that Ralph reached the conclusion that he had no symptoms, or we say that he reached an understanding of what his symptoms were and became able to deal with them effectively. What matters is that Ralph's and my collaborative effort to identify his symptoms, brief as it was, made possible what was, as Ralph said, a very successful psychotherapy.

Ralph's treatment also illustrates very clearly something that is often not so obvious, but that nonetheless always applies. In every successful analytic treatment, a significant part of the work is done by the patient on his or her own, and may never be shared with the analyst. And that is as it should be. An analyst's task isn't to present truth to the patient. An analyst's task is to stimulate a learning process in the patient, by means of which the patient can discover his or her own truth and put it to good use.

3

Helpful Questions

Once an analyst and a patient have agreed about symptoms, they can undertake an investigation that has as its goal symptom relief. Every clinical psychoanalysis is an inquiry, an attempt to answer the questions: What is it about the way the patient constructs his or her experience that causes the patient to suffer? Which of the patient's assumptions, conclusions, and expectations need to be reviewed and revised so as to relieve the patient's distress?

But a clinical psychoanalysis is not *only* an inquiry. Understanding the nature of the problem is only half the task. A remedy has to be provided, as well. The patient has to be helped to find new ways of operating to put in place of old, maladaptive ones. A clinical analyst's job is not merely to *reveal* problematic parts of the patient's mental life; it is also to *alter* problematic parts of the patient's mental life.

In practice, these two aspects of the analyst's job converge. While collaborating with a patient to conduct an inquiry into the nature of the patient's problems, an analyst communicates his or her own point of view, different from the patient's. At times, an analyst may offer his or her ideas explicitly; but even when the analyst is only asking questions, the analyst's questions are informed by his or her particular interests and hypotheses. The patient may agree with the analyst's perspective, may disagree, or may be uncertain about it. Whichever the case, the analyst's input is aimed at helping the patient to extend his or her thinking. Confrontation with a different point of view allows the patient to clarify what his or her own way of constructing reality has been; it helps reveal the problem. At the same time, confrontation with a different point of view allows the patient to consider alternatives to his or her customary ways of thinking; it helps remedy the problem. An analyst communicating his or her own take on a patient's experience often has an investigative and a therapeutic effect, simultaneously.

Common sense, not to mention reasonable modesty, direct an analyst to avoid rushing right in with ideas for the patient to consider. Nonetheless, from the very start of clinical work there are opportunities for an analyst to contribute, respectfully and productively— especially if the analyst offers his or her ideas for what they are: not authoritative, disinterested truths, but inevitably subjective perspectives on the matters at hand. I made several comments to Ralph (see Chapter 2) during our meeting that obviously reflected my own conclusions based on my personal experience. The interactions between Ralph's ways of looking at things and mine were clarifying for him— and therapeutic, as well, as it turned out. Ordinarily, though, productive interactions between the analyst's perspectives and the patient's that occur early in analysis are less conclusive than was the case in Ralph's treatment; they are usually part of a more extended process of defining symptoms and symptom relief, and of beginning to map out areas in need of exploration. Following is an account of the first session of a treatment that went on for several years.

SHEILA

Sheila consulted me because her previous therapies hadn't helped her. In those therapies she developed complex, emotionally charged relationships with her therapists and examined the relationships carefully.

Sheila felt she learned things about herself, but her life had failed to change for the better. What did she want to change about her life? I asked. Sheila wasn't sure: she wasn't sure what she had been looking for from treatment in the past, or what she was looking for now. She knew she wanted to be rescued, but she wasn't certain what she wanted to be rescued from. Loneliness, maybe. She knew that in the past she had used therapy to provide herself with a relationship. Buying a relationship isn't a good reason to be in analysis, she said sadly. I asked Sheila what she thought *would* be a good reason to be in analysis. That's a hard question to answer, she responded.

Sheila rummaged around, discussing her marriage and how it had gone bad. Her ex-husband was an underachiever, dependent and depressed. After a few years, she'd gotten tired of taking care of him. Now she was alone at age fifty, and she wanted to feel more connected to people. But she couldn't say what prevented her from feeling more connected to people. I suggested to Sheila that our first order of business should be to look into her difficulty knowing what it was that she might want to change about herself, what would be a reasonable objective for her therapy. She agreed that might be a useful focus.

Sheila thought about how isolated she felt. She told of an Asian woman, Suzanne, in whom she became interested because she wanted to learn all about Suzanne's culture. As soon as Sheila had learned a good deal about the Asian culture, she lost interest in Suzanne. Sheila began to spend less time with Suzanne, who was hurt by the withdrawal. Sheila felt bad about that. I asked Sheila if she believed that she hadn't the right to follow her real interests. Did she think that her decision not to spend time with Suzanne out of obligation meant she was not a good person? Sheila answered that she assumed she *was* bad for withdrawing from her friend, and Sheila was surprised that I seemed to be questioning her assumption.

Now Sheila began to talk about Carol. Her relationship with Carol was probably the most important one in her life. Sheila had been withdrawing, too, she believed, from Carol, now that Carol was planning to move to the suburbs with her boyfriend. Sheila felt that she was not nice to Carol because Sheila resented the geographical distance Carol's move would create; and she resented, too, Carol's dependence upon her boyfriend. Sheila pursued the idea that she was not nice for resenting Carol in this way. Sheila talked about how controlling she was, noting that she frequently lectured Carol.

I said to Sheila that it might well be helpful for us to question on a pragmatic basis the attitudes that she criticized in herself—to ask whether they contributed to her distress—but I was not sure I understood what she saw as the moral issue involved. Sheila was surprised by my comment and interested in it. She considered the moral dimension of her relationship with Carol. Evidently, Carol was an ex-prostitute who had been very druggy at times in her life. Sheila really got on Carol's case. Sometimes Carol resented it, but she appreciated it, too. To me, it actually sounded like a nice quid pro quo between Sheila and Carol: Sheila got to feel like an important caretaker, and Carol got the care she needed. I said this to Sheila, and she responded by telling me that after attending a Jesuit college, she had entered a convent. She became a nun and was part of an order whose mission was to care for delinquent girls.

Sheila then talked about why she had become a nun. The eldest of six children, she knew she did not want to be barefoot and pregnant like her Catholic mother, nor did she want to submit to her father's intimidating rages. He was a bully, but a charmer. Sheila talked at some length about her father's appeal, as well as about his temper tantrums.

Still, she said, she just did not feel that she was a nice person. She argued with motorists who cut her off, exhibiting a kind of "don't-fuck-with-me" attitude. Sheila felt bad when she did that. It wasn't grown up; she thought she ought to be different. I asked her if she felt like her father when she lost her temper. She certainly did, she said. I pointed out that apparently there were some good things about her father and some bad things. I said I thought that Sheila needed to criticize herself when she imitated bad things about her father, but not when she put to use good things that she learned from him. Deciding which were which was an important sorting process, and not always an easy one.

Sheila agreed, realizing that she had always been on a moral quest when she had been in therapy before. My approach seemed different from her previous analysts': I was practical and direct. But she needed to find some way to feel like a good person, something she had not known how to do since she gave up her religion. She wanted treatment to provide salvation; she wanted treatment to make her feel morally good.

I said that feeling morally good seemed like a very reasonable goal for treatment, but the feeling couldn't be achieved by looking for an authoritative judgment from the analyst. I had the impression that she had been looking for that in her prior treatments. Sheila confirmed this, telling me that she always started out that way, but eventually saw her analyst's clay feet, at which point the analyst's blessing meant nothing to her. I told Sheila that, obviously, in order to feel okay, she would have to be her own authority; there was no other way. If there were traits in herself that she thought were bad, she would have to change them; and if she decided that she disapproved of herself unrealistically, she would need to find out why that happened and change it. Sheila reflected for a while and told me that I was presenting her with a way of thinking about how treatment would save her that was different from before. In her previous treatments, she had bought into the idea that she would be saved by taking a healing journey into her past, guided by the analyst. It never seemed to do any good.

Instead of inviting her to do that, she said, I seemed to be giving her my own ideas, not the same as hers, to consider. The big issue, Sheila said, would be to make sure that she didn't just accept a new dogma from me—she had no desire to become a nun in my church! Thinking about what had happened so far, Sheila decided that the idea that she was burdening herself by moralizing was very helpful.

Now her thoughts turned to the film director Luis Bunuel and his depiction of the Last Supper in *The Discreet Charm of the Bourgeoisie*, where people eat in the bathroom and shit in the dining room. She chuckled, thinking about it. I suggested that perhaps the appeal of the scene in the Bunuel movie was that it showed the absurdity of received morality by turning it on its head. Sheila agreed, and added that she liked Bunuel because of his refusal to accept Catholic orthodoxy. She had the impression that I did not want her to worship in treatment with me; she wished she had worshiped less in previous treatments.

We were nearing the end of our time, and Sheila remarked that she thought it had been a good session. It felt like what we did had been for *her*, not for me. She realized how much she had always deferred to her analysts—at least at the beginning, before they fell off their pedestals. She always assumed that she would have to be in treatment all her life in order to remedy her moral faults. Now she thought she had a choice about whether she even needed to be in treatment at all. Maybe if she thought more often that she had choices, she wouldn't get so angry; and maybe, if she weren't so angry so much of the time, she wouldn't feel like such a bad person. Sheila started crying, aware that at the moment she was more sympathetic to herself than she could remember having been in a long time. She had spent so much of her life feeling resentful about being oppressed, she reflected. That had caused her to get rebellious and disobedient, which only further convinced her that she was a bad person. She had always been angrily trying to break out of prison. Now she thought that maybe the prison had been one of her own making, by moralizing against herself.

The way Sheila presented herself and described her reasons for seeking treatment exemplifies the very common clinical situation in which a patient arrives, feeling in need and asking for help, but having no clear idea of what his or her symptoms are or what a reasonable goal for treatment might be. The most Sheila could say was that she wanted to be rescued from loneliness. She did not know what was causing her to remain lonely; she identified nothing specific about herself that needed to change. As I told Sheila, and it made sense to her, the first thing we had to do was to try to understand why it was so difficult for her to be clearer about what she felt was wrong and what she might expect from treatment. Obviously, I was beginning an inquiry. But I was beginning the inquiry by stating an opinion of my own, and I continued to communicate my opinions, implicitly and explicitly, throughout our meeting.

In an effort to help Sheila become clearer about what her symptoms were and what symptom relief would be, I asked Sheila a number of questions, some of which she could answer and others of which she could not. There were also several times when I pursued our investigation by stating my own personal views—for example, when I told Sheila that she could only feel okay about herself by being her own authority, rather than by seeking the approval of others; or when I said to her that she would have to separate what she wanted to imitate about her father from what she did not. I didn't make value judgments about Sheila, but I did communicate opinions, based on my personal experience, concerning certain matters of importance to her. When I saw things differently than Sheila, it was obvious to her, sometimes even surprising, as when I questioned her assumption that she should feel guilty about spending less time with Suzanne. The interactions between our different points of view proved extremely productive. By the end of the session, Sheila had identified something about herself that she very much wanted to change: she wanted to discontinue her habitual, confining, self-punitive moralizing. And she had developed an idea of how symptom relief would feel: like being released from a prison of her own creation. Sheila hoped to feel freer, and therefore less angry and less rebellious. Sheila was getting clearer about what was wrong and what she was after, and we were on our way.

Traditional conceptions of clinical analytic technique direct the analyst to avoid being too active, especially at the beginning of treatment, and even more especially when activity involves the analyst making his or her own personal ideas known. Furthermore, focusing on symptoms and symptom relief is traditionally considered to be counterproductive because it is thought to encourage the patient to intellectualize, leading away from emotionally significant exploration of the treatment relationship, including transference analysis.

I find none of this to be true, and I think my first meeting with Sheila was an example in point. Actively pursuing with Sheila greater clarity concerning her symptoms and the symptom relief she was seeking, with me contributing my own opinions where they seemed relevant, did not distract Sheila from exploring the influence of past relationships upon her current life. Quite to the contrary, it led her to recognize—and recognize very quickly, all things considered—an identification with her father of which she had previously been unaware. Moreover, Sheila was able to begin to see the role that her identification with her father, and her fear of it, played in her tendency toward harsh self-criticism.

Nor was this an intellectual line of investigation. Actually, it produced an intense affective response in Sheila of a kind of which she had been incapable for a very long time. Sheila began to explore our relationship in an emotionally meaningful way, looking into conflicts brought up by her urge to submit to me as she had submitted to others in the past. She was already engaged in transference analysis par excellence.

One final point about analyst–patient interactions early in treatment. The manner in which the interactions take place establishes, at the very beginning, ground rules that will have a decisive influence on all the work that follows. Consider how lost and confused Sheila claimed to be at the outset, how plaintively passive she was, but how quickly she became an active participant in our investigation. Initially vague and unforthcoming, by the end of the session she was able to articulate what she appreciated about me (the session felt like it was for her), what intrigued her but left her a bit uncertain (my pragmatism), and what worried her (she did not want to be seduced into worshiping in my church). She brought forward these aspects of her experience of our relationship, making them matters we could look into together.

A truly collaborative relationship, with patient and analyst on a level playing field, is a sine qua non for effective analytic treatment. Sheila and I were able to establish such a relationship very quickly. How did that happen, given the far from promising opening of the session? It was crucial that I consistently communicated to Sheila that *she* would define the goals of the treatment, *she* would decide for herself what her symptoms were and what we would aim for as symptom relief; I would not try to install myself as an authority on how she needed to change. A patient will only feel himself or herself to have an authoritative voice in the treatment relationship if the analyst invites it.

Also, a patient will only be truly candid in analytic treatment if the analyst is willing to be equally candid. It was very important that

I explained myself to Sheila as we went along, and did not hesitate to make my own point of view explicit. How a patient appears in treatment depends very much upon context. Initially, Sheila seemed helpless and opaque. Eventually, she revealed herself to be sharp and feisty. The transformation might not have taken place if I, as her analyst, had approached her in a less active and personally direct way or expected her to defer to my expertise.

4

Monitoring Therapeutic Benefit

Consensus about symptoms and symptom relief is required in order for treatment to proceed (see Chapter 3), but the way analyst and patient formulate their goals initially isn't to be taken as absolute, once and for all. If analytic investigation is productive, understanding of the nature of the patient's symptoms evolves; and understanding about the goals of analytic work evolves, correspondingly. Consider, for example, a man who seeks relief from the symptom of constant anxiety. Exploration reveals that his anxiety is inevitable because he sets impossibly high standards for himself and therefore lives in perpetual fear of failure. Because of this realization, the definition of the patient's symptom alters; his experience of anxiety is no longer the target of the investigation. Now it's his tendency to aim unrealistically high that needs to be understood and changed.

Even as the definition of a patient's symptoms evolves with progressive understanding, symptom relief remains the criterion by which analytic work is validated. No matter how compellingly insights achieved account for a patient's distress, and for the patient's experiences, past and present, within and outside the treatment relationship, and no matter how much conviction analyst and patient together develop about those insights, if the insights are not accompanied by demonstrable symptom relief, their validity must be questioned. Despite being convinced about what they have learned, analyst and patient may be on the wrong track; or, at the very least, they may need to add something important to their understanding.

Since symptom relief is the outcome criterion best used to evaluate the success of analytic work, observations concerning whether progress toward symptom relief is taking place need to play an important role in directing analytic technique. Many of the decisions an analyst makes—what to investigate, how to intervene—should be determined by whether the patient is experiencing therapeutic benefit. The following case report illustrates in detail how keeping track of symptom relief guides an analyst's clinical choices.

ELLEN

Ellen, a nurse in her late forties, was depressed. She was depressed because she badly wanted to have a satisfying relationship with a man, but had become convinced that she could never have one. For the past fifteen years, she had stopped even trying. But now, as her fiftieth birthday approached, she felt awful about what seemed destined to be the permanent emptiness of her romantic life. She sought treatment as a last resort, to see if there might be any way to change her bleak prospects.

When she was young, Ellen had not been comfortable with boy–girl socializing. She always felt unattractive and inept. She didn't date at all in high school. In her last year of nursing school, at age twenty-one, she became extremely attracted to Richard, a sixteen-year-old high school student who came to an outpatient clinic where she was working. The fact that she was significantly older than Richard permitted her to feel confident enough to begin a relationship with him. They started to go out, against the strenuous objections of both their families. When Richard graduated, they got married and moved away to San Francisco, where he enrolled in college and she got a job in a hospital.

Ellen found Richard beautiful. She felt that she was completely in love with him and he with her. However, she realized that Richard had some growing up to do. Their marriage was never consummated. Nonetheless, Ellen cherished fantasies of a wonderful future together: Richard would become a successful businessman; they would have children and live in a big house in a nice neighborhood. In fact, Richard did not do very well in his courses. He was undisciplined, got into drugs, and eventually dropped out of college. When, after five years, he asked for a divorce, Ellen reluctantly agreed.

Ellen was ashamed of how unrealistic she had been about Richard. It made her feel even more insecure about herself as a woman. After her divorce, she dated only rarely. She was thrilled when she met Paul, who became smitten with her and pursued her vigorously. Paul was an ardent and experienced lover. With him, Ellen had her first fulfilling sexual experience. Eventually, they moved in together.

Gradually, Paul's sadistic interests, which had always been present, became more and more pronounced. Ellen didn't enjoy the bondage and other dominance–submission games that Paul insisted on, but she went along. She assumed Paul was right when he accused her of being sexually inhibited. When Paul began staying out late, Ellen ignored her suspicions that he was unfaithful. One night, he brought home a lover and suggested a threesome. Ellen refused. She was terribly hurt. In the morning, Paul moved out. Ellen was devastated. After that, she never developed another relationship with a man.

Ellen enjoyed friendships with women, which tended to be carefully selected and intimate. At one point, pessimistic about ever finding happiness with a man, she tried to start a lesbian relationship with a woman about whom she cared deeply; but it just didn't work. Ellen liked sex with a man, and she couldn't get that out of her mind. The lesbian relationship went back to being just a friendship. From then on, after a few desolate one-night stands with men, Ellen's sex life came to consist exclusively of masturbation. Her fantasies usually involved unavailable men of her acquaintance upon whom she developed hopeless, secret crushes—married doctors, or other nurses' husbands.

Ellen saw her terrible self-image as having been caused by her mother's relentless criticism of her throughout her childhood. As far back as Ellen could remember, her mother had held up an image of what Ellen was supposed to be like, and had made it clear to Ellen that she was constantly falling short. When Ellen's mother was on her deathbed and Ellen came to the hospital to say goodbye, her mother turned her face away in disgust, refusing to talk to Ellen or even look at her.

Ellen believed that her father loved her, but this was more of an inference on Ellen's part than an experience of being actively accepted and supported by him. Her father never intervened on her behalf when her mother screamed at her and insulted her. He spent a lot of time at work; and when he was home, he tended to remain hidden behind his newspaper.

Ellen was an only child. There was no sibling with whom she could compare notes. Though she thought that her mother was self-ish and cruel, Ellen concluded that there must be something wrong with her as a daughter for things to have turned out so badly between them. Especially, she had a deep sense that her mother's disappoint-ment in her femininity—Ellen wasn't pretty enough; she didn't know how to behave properly; she was aggressive, hostile, and unladylike—must be valid. After all, her mother, despite all her faults, was a mature woman. She had gotten married and had a child. Ellen felt incapable of doing the same and believed that her mother must be right when she told Ellen she was inadequate.

Our work together centered on trying to understand the reasons for Ellen's inability to free herself from her mother's negative judg-ment. It was my impression that despite her significant criticisms of her mother, Ellen maintained a considerable and costly idealization of her mother, which lent credibility to the accusations with which her mother had bombarded her. As we went over Ellen's view of her childhood, it became increasingly clear that Ellen was powerfully motivated to avoid recognizing what, from her portrayal, seemed to have been her mother's terribly hurtful narcissism. Ellen could tolerate the thought that her mother was abusive, even that her mother hated her; but these perceptions implicitly assumed that her mother was powerfully, if misguidedly, attached to Ellen. It was immeasurably harder for Ellen to consider that, to a significant extent at any rate, her mother simply did not love her—that her mother found no difficulty in placing her own selfish preoccupations ahead of Ellen's needs. The kind of maternal interest, let alone concern for her daughter's welfare, that one might expect to find in a mother was evidently absent in Ellen's mother.

In order to cherish the idea that her mother was passionately, but ambivalently, involved with her, Ellen was obliged to find at least a measure of truth in the image of herself that she saw reflected in her mother's eyes; and the result was exorbitantly costly to Ellen's self-esteem. Our analysis of the problem allowed Ellen to engage in a profoundly painful mourning process. She had to relinquish her image of a turbulent and erratic, but loving and lovable mother. In its place Ellen accepted the realization that her mother had, in crucial ways, failed to love her. Along with the loss, however, came the possibility for Ellen to construct a new, more positive, liberating image of herself. Ellen began to date again. Her self-confidence increased. She no longer avoided trying to find a relationship with a man, which was something she very much wanted.

These changes in Ellen's attitude and behavior concerning men and dating were the first solid evidence of symptom relief that we observed. They confirmed for me that we were on the right track in pursuing the idea that Ellen's idealization of her mother and corresponding depreciation of herself were making it difficult for her to discredit her mother's criticisms.

Now that Ellen was dating again, we had the opportunity to identify many of the ways her habitual expectations—assumptions about who she was, and how others would see her—sabotaged her social life with men. In her relationship with me as well, Ellen was afflicted by doubt. She worried that by encouraging her to think that she could be a desirable woman, I was engaging in wishful thinking, that I was selling her a bill of goods that made me feel more helpful and generous, but was setting her up for bitter disappointment. Alternatively, if I were silent for any time, Ellen would get a panicky feeling that I had lost interest, that I had disappeared, like her father behind his newspaper.

Eventually, Ellen met Howard, a kind and gentle, solid guy, who fell in love with her and let her know it. By now, the analytic work we had done permitted Ellen to recognize, enjoy, and reciprocate Howard's feelings. After a few months, they were spending virtually every night together. Howard's marriage had ended badly several years before, so that he was understandably cautious about rushing into a formal commitment; but everything pointed toward the two of them living together soon, and eventually marrying.

Here was further symptom relief making an appearance. Ellen's ability to enjoy a relationship with a man, to avoid sabotaging it through negative expectations and lack of self-confidence, was something very new. The dramatic change confirmed the work we had done, especially our investigation of Ellen's concerns that I couldn't be trusted; that I was deceiving her and leading her on to an inevitable, horrible disappointment.

Because of her relationship with Howard, Ellen was in seventh heaven. She was extremely grateful to me. After two years of treatment, her dream, which she had come to believe was an impossible dream, was now coming true. She couldn't believe it was happening. And that was the problem. Even though she had what she had always wanted, Ellen remained in the grip of a kind of hypochondria. She feared that she might develop a fatal illness that would cut her down on the eve of her greatest happiness. She made frequent visits to physicians, with morbid anxieties instigated by relatively trivial symptoms. Sometimes, she pressed her doctor to perform diagnostic tests that the doctor assured her were not necessary.

If not a physical illness, Ellen feared, then some other kind of catastrophe would prevent her from being happy. She tortured herself with morbid concerns about Howard. Why hadn't he proposed yet? It must be that his traumatic marriage had left him incapable of entering into another long-term relationship. His love for her was cooling. Because of these disaster fantasies, Ellen required a great deal of reassurance. Howard was willing to provide it, in a loving and patient way; but Ellen never stayed consoled for long. Her needs—not to say demands—went on unabated. There was a danger that, if this problem persisted, Ellen's anxiety about her relationship with Howard failing would turn into a self-fulfilling prophecy.

Now Ellen's distress returned. Instead of feeling increasingly better, she began to feel worse. New symptoms appeared. To me this meant that either we had taken a wrong turn, or that something more needed to be learned.

The question, for us, became: Why couldn't Ellen believe in her good fortune? We had unveiled a number of motivations underlying Ellen's inability to rid herself of her mother's critical view of her. That work had proven extremely useful to Ellen in a variety of ways. But she still felt, she said, that she didn't deserve to be happy. She was sure that something terrible would happen and everything would be ruined. When I asked Ellen what she meant when she said she felt she didn't deserve to be happy, she answered that she felt guilty; but she found it hard to say, specifically, about what.

I encouraged Ellen to pursue her associations. She thought about how rageful she could become. She remembered times that she literally wished that her mother would die. Ellen speculated that she believed that she had somehow caused her mother's fatal cancer. Maybe now she felt doomed to share her mother's fate. To me, it sounded intellectual and formulaic. Ellen's memories of hating her mother, even wishing her dead, were certainly sincere; but Ellen's claims to remorse rang a bit hollow. After all, Ellen knew very well that her mother had been abusive and that her fury toward her mother had been entirely justifiable, under the circumstances. Ellen's idea that she believed that she'd caused her mother's cancer seemed like psychologizing. Ellen was passionately sincere, but I had my doubts. The most important point, to my mind, was that the alleged insight on Ellen's part produced no alleviation of her unrealistic concerns, no amelioration of her urgent, insatiable, and ultimately self-defeating need for reassurance.

Here is an excellent example of how an understanding that I might very well have felt obliged to respect, given that Ellen was so convinced of it, wasn't persuasive because it was not accompanied by symptom relief. And because of that, instead of following the line of investigation Ellen was proposing, our work took another direction.

I began to get annoyed at Ellen. I experienced her as whining. This was most unusual; generally, I felt very warmly toward Ellen and sympathetic to her complaints, even when they were exaggerated. At first, I chalked up my annoyance to my own psychology—to my frustration at having my therapeutic zeal and analytic ambitions thwarted. But then I realized there was more to it. There was something quite narcissistic about Ellen's suffering. She spoke a great deal about how guilty she felt, but essentially she was complaining about feeling guilty. Clearly, Ellen felt very sorry for herself. How guilty does someone really feel if she feels sorry for herself for feeling guilty? Ellen's implication was that her guilt feelings were an unmerited burden.

When I pointed out to Ellen that she described feeling guilty, but always with the implicit judgment that her guilt feelings were undeserved, she got very hurt and angry. Clearly, her sense of comfort and safety with me was disrupted. Now, not infrequently, Ellen would begin a session by telling me that she felt fragile and reluctant to talk, that she was concerned I would criticize her. She admonished me not to be too hard on her. Ellen conveyed that being with me was like being with her mother, that she was suffering in treatment just as she did in the rest of her life. At the same time, Ellen was puzzled by her experience of me as abusive because she believed, from all her prior experience, that I was well intended toward her.

In the course of these developments, my recognition of Ellen's narcissism led me to a corollary observation. Despite all her protests about how guilty she felt, Ellen had never mentioned anything that she actually regretted, concerning which at least some measure of guilty feeling might be realistic. She was certainly aware that her demands for reassurance from Howard and from me were unreasonable, but given their self-defeating nature, they were more a cause for anxiety than for guilt. I thought in particular about Ellen's relationship with Richard. Granted, Ellen's marriage had been an extremely self-defeating step for her; but hadn't it been harmful to Richard, too? Ellen had taken up with a patient in a clinic where she was working, someone considerably younger than herself, and entered into an unsuccessful relationship with him. Didn't she have questions, in retrospect, about the morality of her actions? I'd heard quite a bit from Ellen about the wasted five years of her life and the traumatic effects she experienced; but she'd never once expressed curiosity about what had happened, eventually, to Richard, let alone remorse about how she'd gotten him involved in something that wasn't good for him.

I shared these thoughts with Ellen, and at first she had a hard time understanding what I was talking about. She claimed to feel very guilty about her marriage, but her elaborations of her sense of guilt kept sliding into regret about how wasteful and destructive the marriage had been for her. I pointed out to Ellen how difficult it was for her to think about how she had acted badly toward Richard. I suggested to her that her continuing feeling that she didn't deserve to be happy and her expectations of disaster might stem from an understanding, which she was reluctant to face, that she really had done some things that weren't very nice. While it was true that she had often been a victim in life, it was also true that at times, out of her desperation, she had victimized others.

At this point in the treatment, I introduced an entirely new line of thought that had occurred to me as important. It arose from my response to Ellen's concerns, but it was not something that Ellen herself had considered. Furthermore, my intervention, besides being helpfully intended, was obviously also a criticism of Ellen that expressed my irritation with her. Of course, an analyst's interventions always express the analyst's personal motivations, often unconsciously. Still, this moment in my work with Ellen represents an unusually conspicuous instance of an analyst causing the treatment to dramatically change course on the basis of his own affectively charged reaction (see Chapter 10.) I realized that my intervention would likely produce a strong response in Ellen and might backfire. It was because of the sustained lack of alleviation of Ellen's unrealistic and destructive anxieties that I felt the risk was justified. Because she remained symptomatic, I concluded that we had to search for something new and/or different that could be added to our understanding.

Ellen reacted to what I said by being horrified about herself. For several sessions in a row, she lamented her treatment of Richard, castigated herself, and described complete pessimism about her future—she really was awful and didn't deserve happiness. My impression was that Ellen was beating herself up in a plea for sympathy, in order to ward off genuine self-criticism, in the hope of being reassured by me. I told her so. That was toward the end of a session. What I said brought Ellen up short, and the hour concluded in silence.

Here, as is often the case, we were at sea—I had a notion of what might be a useful line of investigation and I was persevering in it, but with trepidation because there was no symptomatic improvement to confirm the validity of the approach I was taking.

The next time we met, Ellen seemed sober and reflective. She announced that she had a confession to make. This was something about which she felt really terrible, and something about which she had, in effect, lied to me. She knew very well that she had led me to assume that her marriage with Richard had never been consummated because of his immature failure to perform. That wasn't true. In fact, he had tried to penetrate her many times at the beginning of their relationship, but she had been unable to let him. Painfully and haltingly, Ellen described an unremitting vaginismus that had ultimately caused Richard to give up attempting to have sex with her. She knew, she said, that Richard's frustration and hurt had been an important reason for his drug use and failure in college. Ellen began to sob. Richard had taken up riding motorcycles, she told me, and a couple of times had been in terrible accidents. She had been so selfish and so bad for him.

Ellen spent a couple of weeks going over what her marriage had actually been like. She decided that she'd been very screwed up to feel okay about taking advantage of Richard. He was really only a kid when she met him, and she should have restrained herself. She'd been drowning, but the way she tried to save herself wasn't right. She considered trying to get in touch with Richard, to apologize and to find out how he was doing; but ultimately, she decided that it would likely be more disruptive than useful or kind. She thought back to how hard it had been for her to admit that she had been destructively selfish toward Richard when I first raised the idea. That put her in mind of a woman with whom she had felt very close some years ago, who had eventually said that she couldn't be friends any more because Ellen's requirements were just too high. At the time, Ellen had been very hurt and hadn't been able to figure out what her friend was talking about; but now she understood. Ellen remembered how entitled to sympathy she had felt in that relationship, how much attention she had expected.

These insights on Ellen's part impressed me as crucial and moving. They involved a radical change in her view of herself, past and present, which she explored with what seemed to be authentic, even profound, emotion. Nonetheless, while I was encouraged, I was not able to feel certain that we were out of the woods because there was no evidence that Ellen's new understanding had produced significant symptomatic improvement.

As she continued with these painful reflections, Ellen's attitude and behavior toward Howard altered. She began to be keenly aware of his loving patience, grateful for it, and worried about abusing it. More often now, when she became anxious she would make the judgment that she was dealing with an irrational concern, and would try to set it aside on her own instead of asking Howard to reassure her. At the same time, as her misguided sense of entitlement diminished, her legitimate sense of entitlement grew. She acknowledged her sexual inhibitions and challenged them. At her initiative, she and Howard began to be more adventurous in ways they both enjoyed. Now we could see symptom relief that confirmed the validity of the latest phase of our work together.

As time went on, Ellen continued to be able to participate more happily in her relationship with Howard. She and Howard got married. Ellen's susceptibility toward unnecessary worrying didn't disappear completely, but it remained much reduced; and when an exaggerated concern did crop up in her mind, she was usually able to deal with it without laying a trip on Howard or one of her doctors. Eventually, with regard to the symptom relief she hoped to achieve, Ellen felt satisfied and terminated her analysis.

Traditional conceptions of analytic technique specifically direct an analyst *not* to track symptom relief as a guide to technique. They conceptualize the analyst as an authority on clinical process whose expertise grants a perspective on the events of treatment that transcends the patient's judgments concerning his or her state of well-being. So, for example, according to traditional theory, the appearance of new symptoms during treatment is a sign of progress, because it reflects a productive shift in the dynamics of the patient's mental life. My own view of the matter is opposite to the traditional one. For me, the appearance of new symptoms is an indication that something is amiss. Certainly, it's sometimes possible to speculate retrospectively that appearance of new symptoms was part of a storm that could not be avoided. (This may well have been true of Ellen's treatment, for example.) Nonetheless, a downturn in therapeutic benefit to the patient signals a situation that needs to be rectified, not a welcome development. Failure to keep track of therapeutic benefit and to make technical choices on the basis of whether symptom relief is being achieved leaves an analyst wide open to dangerous complacency about his or her work. It spares the analyst accountability at the patient's expense.

Flying Blind

The therapeutic benefit that a patient gains from analytic treatment is the outcome of a learning process. The patient's symptoms arise from maladaptive assumptions, expectations, and ways of dealing with them. When clinical analysis is successful, it is because the patient has learned to revise his or her maladaptive assumptions and expectations, and to develop new coping mechanisms.

One aspect of the learning process is an explicit investigation, conducted collaboratively by patient and analyst. This aspect of the learning process was illustrated, for example, in Ellen's treatment (see Chapter 4), when she and I examined how her idealization of her mother perpetuated Ellen's acceptance of her mother's criticisms; or when we looked into some important, puzzling contradictions concerning Ellen's professed guilt feelings.

At the same time, much of the learning that produces therapeutic benefit takes place through interactions between patient and analyst that are not necessarily discussed, or even consciously identified, but that nonetheless permit the patient to disconfirm old assumptions and expectations and to cope differently than in the past. Alexander and French coined the serviceable term *corrective emotional experience* to describe this kind of interaction. For example, it was a corrective emotional experience for Ellen when she complained resentfully to me about the way she felt I was treating her and found that I, unlike her mother, tolerated the criticism and continued to have Ellen's welfare as my first priority.

Traditional theories of psychoanalytic process disparage corrective emotional experiences as being merely "transference cures" or "flights into health." According to traditional theories, valid psychoanalytic learning consists exclusively of "insights" that are consciously formulated in words by patient and analyst during their dialogue. On the other hand, experienced clinical analysts know very well that in every successful treatment, many of the factors that produce symptom relief are not consciously identified and never come up for discussion. It is quite common for so-called transference cures and flights into health to endure and to constitute a significant part of the therapeutic benefit gained from analysis. All in all, it's fair to say that a successful analytic treatment is based upon a sequence of corrective emotional experiences, only some of which may come to be recognized, let alone explicitly investigated.

There is usually significant overlap between explicit and implicit learning during a successful psychoanalysis. A particular part of the explicit investigation that analyst and patient carry out together may function implicitly as a corrective emotional experience for the patient—let's say, for instance, if the analyst is respectfully interested in what a patient thinks and feels, whereas important people in the patient's past were not. At the same time, when patient and analyst become aware of what has been an implicit corrective emotional experience for the patient and discuss it explicitly, the discussion contributes to the investigation that they are carrying out together.

So, it isn't very difficult to know in general terms what must happen for analytic treatment to be successful. The problem, however, is that knowing in *general* terms doesn't take us very far. *Particular* corrective emotional experiences are needed if treatment is to be successful. How can an analyst know *specifically* what is required in order for a given patient to find symptom relief? As an analytic treatment proceeds, the analyst sometimes recognizes *after the fact* that a sequence of clinical events has been a corrective emotional experience for the patient. But it would be dangerously presumptuous for an analyst to think that he or she can know *in advance* what will be a corrective emotional experience.

Furthermore, there is the problem of how to arrange for a corrective emotional experience to take place. Even if an analyst could know which corrective emotional experiences to provide for a patient, how would the analyst provide them? By role playing? That sort of contrivance never achieves its intended purpose. The circumstances of analytic treatment are very intimate, and a patient can't help but perceive when an analyst is being inauthentic. Artificiality and imposture go against the fundamental ethic of candor that is essential to a productive analytic encounter. Role playing, no matter how well intentioned, will defeat its own purposes.

As far as corrective emotional experiences are concerned, an analyst never knows ahead of time exactly where he or she needs to go or how to get there. In that sense, an analyst is always flying blind. Nonetheless, if an analyst acknowledges flying blind, there are approaches to the situation that can help the analyst collaborate with a patient to find useful directions in which to proceed as they go along. The following case report illustrates such a collaboration. It describes a clinical experience I had some time ago that influenced my thinking about how best to fly blind as an analyst.

LAURA

Laura was a woman in her early thirties who came to see me, complaining that she felt like she was falling down a well and couldn't do anything about it. That was all she could say about her distress. I tried to get Laura to elaborate, explaining why it would be helpful for her to say anything at all that came to mind about her experience, but to no avail. "I just feel like I'm falling down a well, and I can't do anything about it," she repeated. She remained very concrete in her statements, though she clearly understood what I meant when I talked to her about her use of metaphor.

In fact, I couldn't help Laura speak spontaneously about very much at all. For the most part, she responded only to questions from me, and then usually after a significant pause. Sometimes her silence lasted long enough that I wondered whether she intended not to answer, or had become distracted; but eventually she would speak, and what she said was invariably to the point. It was apparent that she took time to consider and carefully choose her words. Any number of efforts on my part to explore with Laura the reasons for what was obviously a drastic caution on her part were in vain.

Slender and pale, she sat quite still in her chair, her drawn features composed in a grave expression. There was no doubt of her suffering and her desire for help. She took our dialogue quite seriously, but she was determined to participate in it in her own way. Was Laura paranoid? It certainly seemed so. Did she have a thought disorder? Not in the sense of any difficulty with abstract thinking or concentration, at any rate, though she very well might have been delusional. I found Laura poignant and appealing. Something about her intelligent and purposeful vigilance, extreme as it was, gave me the sense that I might be able to help her gain some relief through an understanding of her suffering, if I could find a way to negotiate a partnership with her.

Over several sessions, I questioned Laura about her problem and what had led up to it, and tried to gain an impression of her history. There were definite limits to what she was willing to reveal; and I soon learned that when she decided to go no further on a given topic, it was pointless to try to make her reticence a subject for investigation. The following picture emerged.

The eldest of five, Laura had been raised in relative affluence on the East Coast. Her father was a very successful businessman and her mother a socialite. The parents were preoccupied with their own interests. She had never felt close to either of them, nor to her younger brother and sisters. When she graduated from high school at seventeen, she left home to live independently and had been completely out of contact with her family ever since. She would say no more about her childhood.

She had taught herself to type, and after leaving home supported herself largely through office work. She was evidently a very efficient secretary and had no trouble finding jobs. She moved a number of times—at one point, she spent a year in Alaska because she wanted to see what it was like to live in a less developed place—and wound up in the Bay Area, where she decided to go to college. She majored in classics, and graduated from university summa cum laude. She then went on to a prestigious law school, finishing second in her class. She chose the law because she liked solving logical problems. She thought of becoming a criminal attorney since she felt it was important for people to have their rights—an obviously significant sentiment about which, unsurprisingly, she would say nothing further.

I had the impression that throughout her travels, Laura had remained socially quite isolated, spending much time in solitary pursuits. I did get a glimmer, though, of a few carefully selected, often quite odd relationships with other people. One of these was with a brilliant, eccentric young philosophy-student-turned-car-mechanic, with whom she eventually moved in, and, during her first year of law school, married. The two shared several passionate intellectual interests, including archeology. They spent vacations visiting Indian ruins in this country and in Central and Latin America.

They fought a great deal. Her husband didn't like it when she talked about law school. He also insisted that he should be able to bring his lovers, male and female, to their home. Her resentment of his infidelity led to her complete withdrawal from their sex life, which had previously been active, though she claimed not to have enjoyed it. At the time she first consulted me, they had arrived at an arrangement in which her husband conducted his affairs outside the home and didn't tell her about them. She remained sexually inactive and steadfastly refused her husband's overtures, which had become relatively infrequent.

It seemed to me that Laura's very unusual, and in many ways quite unsatisfying, marriage was of the greatest importance to her. Even when she was most bitterly critical in her descriptions of her husband, she never mentioned a thought of leaving him. When I asked her about this, she would say, "We're married." I inferred that the relationship was a crucial anchor for her.

It was upon graduation from law school, six months prior to our first visit, that the feeling of falling down a well had begun. I learned that despite her great academic success, and her successful history of employment as a secretary, Laura had found herself completely unable to look for a legal position. She had not made a single phone call to set up an interview since graduation. Recently, she had begun to go out less and less for any reason. Increasingly, she dreaded leaving her apartment.

Laura was clearly nursing an acute, fulminating agoraphobia. The timing of its onset suggested that, whatever else was involved, she was intensely conflicted about working as a lawyer. Though I knew really very little about this young woman, I was quite struck by how much importance she seemed to place on her very few, almost irrevocable commitments. A career in law, for which she had worked long and hard, was one; her marriage was another. Taking my cue from her mention in passing that her husband didn't like it when she talked about law school, and given that she portrayed him as extremely narcissistic, competitive, and controlling, I wondered whether she might be struggling with the fear that she would be forced to give up her husband or her profession—either way an insupportable loss. At the end of a session, I said something about this possible dilemma to her, connecting it with her feeling that she was falling down a well and couldn't do anything about it.

Next hour, Laura said that she had made some phone calls and was starting to set up employment interviews. She had also gone out shopping for new clothes. This considerable alleviation of her symptoms was reported very straightforwardly, without significant affect. "I'm happy about it," she stated simply and flatly when I inquired into her manifest lack of feeling about the dramatic change. She did not relate it to what I had said to her the previous hour about a possible conflict with her husband. "I guess so," was her answer when I asked if she thought there might be a connection.

On her way out, Laura surprised me by pausing at the door, turning, and saying—still with the same serious demeanor—"How about giving me a hug?" Somewhat taken aback, I replied, "I don't think that's really the best way I can help you. Let's talk about it next time." My tone was friendly, if anything a bit gently reassuring, since I was concerned she might be hurt by a refusal on my part that we had no chance to discuss.

At our next appointment, Laura came in, sat down, and asked angrily, "Why did you yell at me?" She explained she was referring to the exchange at the door. I tried to invite her to explore her own ideas about why I might have yelled; but of course her position was, "I haven't got the faintest idea, that's exactly why I want you to tell me." I tried to explain that, in my view, I hadn't yelled. I tried to suggest various anxieties or wishes on her part that may have disposed her to experience me as yelling. I tried many things, but none of them accomplished much.

After this turn of events, Laura said even less during our meetings, spending much of her time in tight-lipped silence. Nothing I could do seemed to affect the situation. "Tell you everything that comes to my mind? Why on earth would I want to do that?" she asked derisively. At the same time, she reported that she was moving ahead in her job search. Whatever it was that was going on between us, it seemed to be having a beneficial effect on the rest of her life, so I decided to be patient.

However, as weeks went by, although she continued to progress on the career front, things seemed to get worse and worse during the hours. "I'm a group of particles that will fly apart. I need to be inside you. But you don't want me to be inside you. You're afraid I'll devour you." These thoughts came out a bit at a time. Needless to say, there was no question of further exploration of them. Her fury mounted. Each time she reached into her handbag, I half expected her to produce a .357 magnum or, at the very least, a tape recorder.

My concern steadily increased. I thought there was a real possibility that something dramatic could eventuate. Whatever the therapeutic benefits, some kind of malignant experience of me seemed to be escalating, and I could find no way to address it. I tried to talk to Laura about what seemed to be happening. She just became more and more desperate to have something from me that I didn't know how to provide, and more and more enraged at me for not providing it. I wondered whether, since she was evidently unable to consider relinquishing her painful attachment to me, it might be in her best interests for me to sever it. At the same time, I worried that if I did that, Laura would feel herself a rejected, devouring monster and be utterly devastated.

Finally, one day I said to her: "You know, as we've discussed, I really don't know how to help you. I've explained the ways I usually work with people that I've found to be useful, and they don't make sense to you. I know what you say you want from me; but I don't really understand it, and I haven't been able to make it happen. I worry that by continuing to see you, I'm preventing you from getting into a treatment that might be helpful; I worry that I may even be making you worse. On one hand, you seem to be getting on better with looking for a job than you were before we started; and if our meetings are helpful to you, even if it's in a way I don't understand, I'm happy to continue. But on the other hand, our relationship is causing you tremendous pain, and it seems to be getting worse. Sometimes I think it might be best for you to stop, and that you're unable to yourself, so maybe I should call it off from my end. It's a real dilemma, and I'm not sure how to proceed." To all of this, she said, predictably, nothing.

Laura came in the following session, however, carrying a large stack of spiral-bound notebooks. "I thought these might be useful to you in helping you make your decisions," she announced as she offered them to me. Taken aback by this most unexpected gesture, I accepted them and looked through them. Each line on each page of each book was filled with her small, neat handwriting. What the notebooks contained was a complete record of all our meetings—not only of everything she had said and I had said, reconstructed after each session, but of all the thoughts that had passed through her mind during her silences. I thanked her at length for bringing me the books, and acknowledged how meaningful and important it was that she had decided to let me see them. I told her I wanted to read them all, but it would probably take me a while to do it.

During the hours that followed, Laura frequently asked me if I had finished reading the notebooks yet, and I would reply that I was working on it. As I did make my way through the notebooks, I found that there were no real surprises in what I read. The thoughts that had filled her silences, I saw, were essentially extensions of what she said to me: the same complaints, anxieties, perplexities, and resentments.

Finally, I finished. When I returned the notebooks, I said to her, "I'm very glad you gave me these. In a way, I didn't find anything new. The thoughts you didn't tell me during our meetings seem to me very much in line with the ones you did tell me. After reading everything you wrote, I still don't know how to help you, or if I can help you. But there is one very important thing I did learn from your notebooks: it's clear to me that no matter what my actual intention or how carefully I explained it to you, if I were to unilaterally end the treatment, you would be sure it was because I want to get rid of you, because I don't want you to devour me. That's not the case; I don't want you to think that. So I'm making you a promise here and now: Unless you make it impossible for me to continue by breaking up the furniture or something like that, I'm never going to terminate our meetings on my own initiative."

A small smile crossed Laura's face. After that, her mood in the hours lightened, and she began talking a bit more freely. In time she told me how when she was a child her parents would go off for month-long vacations without warning, leaving it to a babysitter to inform the children when they arrived home from school; how her father sometimes stroked her "little titties," as he called them, when he came into her room to say good night; how conditions of neglect and arbitrariness sparked bitter rivalries among all the siblings; and many other details of what seemed to have been an erratic and abusive upbringing. As always, there remained limits to what she was willing to discuss about the things she disclosed. Meanwhile, Laura was able to find a position as an associate in a law firm, and to realize after a year that it was not a good situation and leave it for a different one. She brought her professional problems up for us to talk about—again, within limits that she established without explanation.

Eventually, Laura and I came into conflict over my policy about cancellations. At that time, I charged for all unfilled missed visits that could not be rescheduled. Laura considered this unfair—not a justifiable way of doing things that she simply didn't like, a different opinion than hers to which I had a right, but manifestly, unequivocally unfair. I saw that her point of view was not going to change. She might have submitted, but she clearly felt she shouldn't have to. I told her I thought I had a perfect right to do things my way and that I disagreed with what I regarded as her self-righteousness, but that our relationship was more important to me than either the principle or the money. I suggested that we compromise. She agreed, proposing that she not be responsible for absences she told me about two weeks or more ahead of time. I accepted this arrangement.

Laura's career proceeded well. Eventually, she found a job she liked a lot. She came to be highly regarded by both her associates and her clients. Along the way she discussed with me such problems as sometimes feeling overidentified with the criminal defendants she represented, and how this interfered with her work. Also, things were changing significantly in her marriage. She had an affair with a colleague, terminated it, and began to confront her husband more directly and constructively with her dissatisfactions. Her husband stopped being unfaithful. They began to forge a more effective day-to-day relationship and resumed having sex.

One day, after we had been working together about two years, Laura came in and announced, "I can't see you." I asked her what she meant (we met vis-à-vis), but she replied only, "I can't see you when you're looking at me." Expectably, further analysis proved impossible. "What do you think we should do?" I asked eventually. "Well," she said, "I think you should face away from me so I can see you." "Sorry," I replied, "I'm not willing to do that." "Why not?" she asked. "Because I don't like working with people when I can't see them," I explained. "How do you think I feel?" she responded. I told her I was sure she didn't like it either. I was very sympathetic, but I just wasn't willing to do what she wanted. She told me that wasn't fair. I said maybe not, but I just wasn't willing. She kept coming to our appointments, though she obviously didn't like the conditions. After a few days of growing discomfort on my part, I said, "Okay. I'm willing to face off to the side and not look at you every other session. How does that sound?" She thanked me, and from then on, that's how we proceeded.

Later, Laura reported that she had re-contacted her family and was beginning to have regular visits with them. She described her mixed feelings toward her affectionate but disorganized and irresponsible mother, and her conflicts in dealing with her brilliant, interesting, and exploitive father. Her social circle widened and I began to hear more about the details of her friendships. She brought forward various ideas about me and feelings toward me. Upon occasion, we were able to relate these to longstanding concerns originating in prior relationships.

At a certain point, Laura again became preoccupied with her experience of me as rejecting. This time she was less furious, and more able to advance her complaint as something to be discussed. Specifically, she said she didn't feel like talking to me because she never got a response to anything she said. I found this particularly puzzling, as I told her, because my own experience was of prizing her sparse communications and of always responding immediately, usually in the hope of helping her say more. Apparently, our views were different, and we didn't seem to be able to get very far in understanding why. We kept on trying to clarify what was happening; but as the months went by, things remained pretty much the same. She didn't feel she got anywhere talking to me about her difficulty in talking to me.

Apparently, we had reached an impasse. Laura didn't like what was happening, but she didn't want to stop seeing me. She just wanted me to change. She was beginning to have the feeling of falling down a well. Once again, I worried that it made no sense to continue our meetings; and once again felt at the same time that it would be a mistake for me to terminate. I told Laura that I was in the same dilemma as before. (Also not for the first time, I went to colleagues for consultation about the case. I received a great deal of sympathy and encouragement, but no enlightenment about how to proceed.)

She wouldn't talk to me about myself because she believed I was unable to listen, but she didn't want to give me up. An idea occurred to me: What about finding her someone else to talk to about me and our relationship? I asked her if she might want to see a second therapist to discuss what was going on with us. She thought it was a good idea and asked me to suggest someone, which I did. Actually, she saw a number of therapists whom I recommended—all women, at her request—for anywhere from one session to three months, until finally she found someone who really worked for her. She settled into a schedule of seeing me three times a week and the other therapist once a week or every other week. This dual therapy continued for the rest of the time we worked together.

Our treatment lasted for two more years, until Laura's husband, who had now returned to graduate school, found a teaching position in another city. When she left, Laura was planning to try to have a baby. She had always felt that it was pointless to bring a child into the world, but as a result of many issues we discussed together, her attitude changed. Over the years since I last saw her, I received a number postcards telling me—always laconically—that things were okay.

Laura's treatment was dramatically successful. The panic and agoraphobia that were her original complaints cleared up completely. Besides her presenting symptoms, Laura's longstanding social isolation diminished, she became more at ease with people, and she developed a circle of friends. Instead of participating passively and resentfully in her marriage, she was able to actively pursue her own interests and to create a more satisfying relationship with her husband. Her habitual pessimism about life changed to the extent that she planned to have children, something she could never even consider before. After completely avoiding her family of origin for almost twenty years, she reestablished contact with them. Clearly, Laura was able to achieve very significant symptom relief that included alteration of an array of maladaptive attitudes and behaviors.

Obviously, Laura and I achieved our fine results without having very much explicit investigative dialogue at all. Initially, I did make an important comment to Laura that connected her distress to a conflict between fear of losing her career and fear of losing her husband; and then, in the later stages of our work, we were able to have conversations in which we looked into Laura's problems in depth together. But most of the time, Laura completely refused to collaborate with me on an inquiry into her psychology. The positive outcome of Laura's clinical analysis was the result of a sequence of largely undiscussed corrective emotional experiences.

Knowing what eventually came to light about Laura's background, it is possible to infer with some confidence ex post facto the nature of the corrective emotional experiences that underlay the success of her treatment. Laura's parents consistently put their own interests well ahead of the interests of their children, whereas I was plainly willing to put up with all sorts of conditions I did not prefer for the sake of Laura's welfare. Laura could see that I did not assume that my agenda would determine what happened between us—even when it was an agenda in which I strongly believed. This, too, was completely different from the way Laura was treated growing up. I was willing to grant Laura significant power within our relationship, something her parents did not come close to doing. I felt an obligation always to explain to Laura what I was doing and what my intentions were. Her parents often acted arbitrarily, without giving reasons for what they did.

However, retrospective understanding is one thing, prospective understanding another. At the beginning I knew next to nothing about Laura's history. I had to find a way to approach her that gave us the best chance to negotiate a successful collaboration without knowing very much at all about her desires or fears. Laura was uncooperative and I was flying blind. Yet, we found our way to the necessary corrective emotional experiences and a happy outcome. Two features of our route to success stand out.

The first was made conspicuous by a turning point—perhaps *the* turning point—in our work together. Outside her treatment, Laura's life was improving, but during our meetings she suffered increasingly in a truly alarming way. I could find no way to ameliorate Laura's escalating distress. I was very worried about continuing with her, but I was equally worried about discontinuing. Not knowing what else to do, I described my dilemma to Laura—and that made all the difference. Laura had no interest in talking with me about herself because she didn't think I knew anything about her. The only statements I could make that she trusted and found useful were statements that I made about myself. What Laura wanted and needed from me was an account of *my own experience of being with her*.

The condition that was unmistakably true for Laura is true for all patients, even if it isn't always obvious. The only thing an analyst really has to offer, and the only thing a patient can really use, is the analyst's account of his or her experience—especially the analyst's account of his or her experience of the events of treatment. When treating patients who are less determined than Laura was to keep the analyst honest, an analyst can very easily get caught up in the mistaken idea that he or she knows about the patient and can lose sight of the fact that all an analyst can actually know about is his or her own experience of being with the patient.

For example, a young man in analysis tells me that I misunderstood something he said. He speaks loudly, and his face turns red. "You seem angry," I comment. A very reasonable remark, one with which any observer would probably agree. Perhaps the patient would agree that he's angry, though he hasn't mentioned it so far. The point is, however, that while I have made what appears to be a comment about *the patient*, if we are meticulously accurate we have to acknowledge that what I am actually doing is stating an inference based on *my own experience*: I note the patient's loud voice and red face; I recall times when I was angry and spoke loudly and got red in the face; I recall times when others have spoken loudly and gotten red in the face, when they turned out to be angry; and so on. From my experience of being with the patient, plus memories of past experiences, I conclude that the patient is very likely angry.

In this instance, the distinction between knowing about a patient and knowing about one's own experience of being with a patient may seem academic and inconsequential. However, there are many clinical situations in which keeping it in mind makes all the difference. It was only because of Laura's fanatical insistence that I realized and acknowledged that I knew nothing about her and could only speak to my own experience. Still, it was that realization and acknowledgment that permitted us to extricate ourselves from a catastrophic downward spiral and go on to work together very successfully. Even with patients who are much more adaptable and forthcoming than Laura was, an analyst's clarity about the nature and the limits of his or her knowledge and expertise makes a decisive difference to the success of the treatment. If an analyst believes himself or herself to be an expert about the patient, the analyst assumes an undeserved authority that will constrain the possibilities for interaction. Then it is far less likely that analyst and patient will find their way to needed corrective emotional experiences.

The second conspicuous feature of the route to success in Laura's treatment is my acceptance of her as a full collaborator. Again, the extremity of Laura's determination was responsible. Prior to treating Laura, I had thought of myself as a rather open and flexible analyst who always invited and considered my patients' ideas about how we might work best together. But Laura made me realize how much further I had to go. My invitations to patients had always been for input about how best to work together within limits dictated by *my* assumptions. In Laura's treatment, for the first time I granted the patient a voice equal to my own in determining the methods we would use— and I only did it because I couldn't think of anything else to do under the circumstances! Subsequently, however, it became fundamental to my approach in every treatment.

If an analyst acknowledges that he or she cannot know in advance which particular corrective emotional experiences a patient needs, then the analyst will realize that there are very definite limitations upon how much he or she, alone, can know about what to do in any given treatment. Therefore, when figuring out how to proceed, it is crucial that the analyst solicit as much help as possible from the patient. Not only is it best for an analyst to take an experimental approach to technique, but the analyst needs to authorize the patient as a full collaborator in experimentation.

6

Playing Your Cards Face Up

Collaborating with a patient about procedure doesn't often require the kind of dramatic innovations that Laura demanded (see Chapter 5). Ordinarily, it's more a matter of soliciting and respecting the patient's input when deciding about frequency of meetings, duration of treatment, and the like, instead of assuming that the analyst knows best about format and that the patient is "resisting" if he or she disagrees. In any case, the most important aspects of collaboration extend beyond decisions about procedure. Effective collaboration requires an analyst to recognize the utility of a patient's observations and suggestions concerning every aspect of the analyst's participation in treatment.

There is no way for an analyst to avoid having blind spots. Each moment of an analyst's activity is determined to a significant degree by factors that remain unconscious no matter how assiduous the analyst's continuing efforts at self-observation and self-analysis. Consultation with colleagues is very helpful, but an analyst only seeks consultation from colleagues when the analyst is aware of a need for consultation; also, even the shrewdest consultant can only deal with what the analyst reports about what has happened in treatment. On the other hand, a patient is in a position to observe his or her analyst closely and continuously, to offer consultation even when the analyst doesn't recognize a need for it, and to comment on features of the analyst's participation that the analyst doesn't notice and therefore couldn't describe to a colleague. At its best, the collaborative working relationship between analyst and patient is reciprocal, in the sense that not only does the analyst point out things to the patient about himself or herself of which the patient is unaware, but the patient points out things to the analyst about himself or herself of which the analyst is unaware. Increased awareness on both sides facilitates the investigation that analyst and patient are carrying out together, and maximizes productive interaction between the two.

In order for a patient to remain willing and able to be a consultant to an analyst, the patient has to know that the consultation he or she offers will be taken seriously; and in order for that to happen, the analyst cannot adopt a traditional posture of analytic anonymity, keeping his or her own experience of the events of treatment private. If a patient calls an analyst's attention to aspects of his or her participation in treatment that the patient feels are significant, and the analyst, instead of giving a candid personal response to the patient's observations, encourages the patient toward further self-reflection, the patient learns that offering observations about the analyst will not be interpersonally consequential, and the patient becomes disinclined to offer them. When an analyst is unwilling to pursue a candid exchange of views with a patient, the patient concludes that the analyst is not really interested in receiving consultation. Collaboration requires that the analyst's actual behavior be a legitimate topic for explicit discussion. Not only the patient's perceptions of the analyst, but the analyst's perceptions of himself or herself as well need to be put on the table. Then, comparison, contrast, and dialectical interaction can occur.

In other words, collaboration between analyst and patient depends upon the analyst playing his or her cards face up. Since an analyst's experience of the events of treatment is shaped by the analyst's personal psychology, an analyst being willing to make his or her experience of treatment available to a patient requires the analyst to be willing to say a good deal about himself or herself—sometimes more than is comfortable. Nor can the policy of playing one's cards face up apply only if the analyst is called upon to respond to inquiry or comment from the patient. An analyst has to take the initiative in playing his or her cards face up. By explaining what he or she is doing and why, the analyst establishes ground rules for the treatment relationship. When an analyst volunteers his or her personal experience of the treatment for the patient's use, it indicates that the analyst regards his or her actual participation as something that can and should be explicitly discussed. In that way, the patient's full collaboration is invited, not just in word but in deed.

ANNE

Anne came to see me because of her inability to feel satisfied in her marriage. As we looked into her problem, I noticed that Anne would relinquish critical thoughts about her husband every time they arose, turning to self-doubt instead. I pointed this out to her. Anne told me that in childhood she had experienced her mother as loving, but quite controlling and intolerant of independence, let alone contradiction, from her children. We discussed the possibility that Anne's reluctance to criticize her husband was based upon a sense of danger that she had learned in relation to her mother.

Anne was a TV journalist whose career was really starting to take off. During one of our meetings, she described how her husband had seemed conspicuously uninterested the evening before when she was telling him, with great excitement, about a story she was working on. Anne considered that her husband might be threatened by her success; but after thinking about that for a while, she decided instead that there must have been something about the way she had been talking to her husband that turned him off.

Listening to her account of the incident and her reflections about it, I said, "I'm confused. What gives you the impression that your way of talking turned your husband off?" Anne responded, with slight irritation, "I don't think you're confused, Owen. I think you have a

view of what's going on. Why don't you just say what you think?"
Well, of course, Anne was right. I wasn't really confused. My hypothesis was that Anne had, as usual, felt the need to criticize herself instead of her husband. However, I wasn't certain that Anne was abdicating her critical capacities, and so I expressed myself inconclusively in order to leave room for the possibility that in this instance perhaps she had perceived something about herself that warranted criticism. I explained this to Anne.

She considered. "That makes sense," she said. "I can understand where you were coming from. But why didn't you just explain your concerns? Instead, you presented yourself as confused, and that wasn't really true—not to mention that it goes against your policy, which you've explained to me, of making your thinking explicit so that we can discuss it if we need to. Not that it's such a big deal, but why did you bullshit like that?"

Good question, I thought, and said as much to Anne. I told her what came to my mind: I was aware of not wanting to seem controlling like Anne's mother. The kind of presumptuousness that Anne felt she got from her mother was something I didn't think Anne needed any more of and was something that I, personally, particularly disliked; therefore, I was taking pains to be sure Anne experienced me as anything but presumptuous. As the hour ended, I was thinking out loud in this vein in response to Anne's question.

The next time we met, Anne began by saying how useful the previous session had been. She was curious about my personal reasons for reacting as I did; but the really interesting thing to her, the more she thought about it, was that I had been, in a way, intimidated by her—sufficiently concerned about her disapproval that I even misrepresented myself! She had never considered that I might be worried about her opinion of me. She always thought of me as completely self-confident and self-sufficient. She thought of her husband in the same way, but revising her view of me made her question her view of him too. Last evening she described to her husband what had happened in her analysis and asked him whether he worried about having her approval. He told her he did. For example, he said, when she talked about her work, he was very reluctant to say anything because when he did, she frequently seemed to think that he was leaping to conclusions about what she was telling him.

So, Anne pointed out to me, there *was* something she did that made other people back off from her. In that sense, she had been right the day before when she had distrusted the idea that her husband was too competitive to be interested in her work, and had wondered instead whether something about her way of talking to her husband had been the problem. Similarly, Anne went on, whatever my susceptibilities were, she realized that she had played a role in my becoming so careful with her that I pretended to be confused when I wasn't. Anne continued to elaborate how useful it had been for her to recognize that she could inadvertently intimidate other people by communicating her exaggerated sensitivities. She and her husband had gone on to have a very long talk about it last night, and afterward they'd made love more intimately and passionately than they had in years. Sexually, too, Anne felt, she'd been shutting her husband down without realizing it. Obviously, she concluded, she was too ready to assume that the people she cared about would treat her the way her mother had, and this expectation was having unintended, destructive effects in her personal relationships.

This vignette illustrates what I mean by playing your cards face up as an analyst. At a couple of points during the session, Anne asked me, essentially, what I thought I was doing: first when she challenged my statement that I was confused; then, after I explained my understanding of why I'd said that I was confused, when she pressed me to explain my motivation for misrepresenting my state of mind. Each time Anne asked for my view of what I was up to, I gave it to her. I didn't decline to answer her questions, or defer answering them, suggesting that Anne first reflect upon her reasons for asking. Instead, I responded to her inquiry as a constructive request for information that would be useful for her to consider, and we took it from there. Clearly, I was not striving for even relative anonymity. My aim was to be as explicit as possible about my own view of my participation in the events of treatment.

The exchange between Anne and me was the consequence of my having played my cards face up consistently, from the beginning, in my work with her. Anne was obviously quite uninhibited about confronting me with her observations and inferences concerning my actions. The reason for Anne's confidence was that she knew from experience that if she did confront me with her observations, she would get an accounting from me about them and we would continue to discuss what we were doing, as each of us saw it, as long as that discussion seemed useful. Had I customarily declined to explain myself, or done so only very cautiously and selectively, or suggested that Anne first reflect upon the motivations that lay behind her questions, Anne would not have felt free to inquire into my view of my own activity in the spontaneous way that she did.

One reason analysts have traditionally been reluctant to share their own experiences of the events of treatment with their patients is that analysts fear creating an undue focus of attention upon themselves at their patients' expense. The concern is reasonable, but in fact it works in exactly the opposite way: the more an analyst acknowledges and is willing to discuss his or her personal participation in the treatment situation, the less room the analyst takes up and the more he or she leaves for the patient. A reticent analyst looms large, occupying center stage as a mysterious object of interest. The patient remains very well aware of being engaged in an encounter with another individual human being; and the patient's need to know the analyst's intentions, assumptions, values—the patient's need to know about the person with whom he or she is actually dealing—does not go away, even if the analyst declares it irrelevant or an interference. When an analyst tries to remain even relatively anonymous, a game of "Guess What's on My Mind" is initiated. Too many patients have wasted too much time in traditionally conducted analytic treatments playing that game. An analyst's willingness to share his or her thoughts helps the analyst *avoid* becoming the focus of attention.

In my work with Anne, I shared with her my own experience of the events of treatment. Anne generally found that helpful; and when she felt otherwise, she did something about it. Because our ground rules were such that Anne could rely on me regarding her opinions about how we should proceed as important contributions, she and I were able to collaborate on the nature and extent of my self-disclosure. Sometimes Anne asked me to say more about what was on my mind; at other times, she judged that it was not useful for her to hear about my thinking in detail. Anne established her own need to know, and it worked out very well.

An analyst playing his or her cards face up encourages the patient to feel free to ask the analyst to explain himself or herself further when the patient thinks that would be useful, or to say less when the patient thinks the analyst is talking too much; and the analyst can, in turn, inquire into the patient's motivations when the patient seems to be either excessively interested in the analyst's experience, or when the patient seems conspicuously incurious about the analyst's experience. An analyst playing his or her cards face up encourages the bilateral candor that is crucial to effective collaboration.

Another reason that analysts have avoided playing their cards face up is a concern that to do so poses an obstacle to the analysis of transference—investigation of the way a patient's experience of past relationships influences the patient's experience of present relationships, especially the patient's experience of his or her relationship with the analyst. The assumption is that if the patient knows what the analyst is really like, opportunities for the patient to fantasize about the analyst and to explore the origins of those fantasies will be foreclosed. That assumption is not supported by clinical evidence. For example, Anne learning from me that I was intimidated by her did not prevent her from fantasizing; quite to the contrary, it *caused* her to become aware that she had always had a fantasy, of which she had not been conscious, that I was completely self-confident and self-sufficient.

If we think about it, the traditional concern about foreclosing opportunities for transference analysis is odd, given how well we know that manifestations of transference are not very easily suppressed. In fact, trying to prevent transference from manifesting itself would be rather like trying to catch a falling safe. I remember a psychiatrist I once treated who, because he was professionally envious of me, needed to console himself with the idea that, busy as I was, I must be neglectful of my family. When he and I met at a parents' meeting at the school it turned out both our children were attending, he was sure that my presence was only a token gesture—the one evening a year I devoted to being a father. Later, when he heard from mutual friends that I went to all my daughter's soccer games, he thought to himself that of course I was only capable of a narcissistic interest in her athletic achievements. He found out about a special holiday dinner that I cooked for the family, and decided that I was just showing off. And so on. So much for a patient knowing about the analyst foreclosing opportunities for the patient's transference fantasies to manifest themselves!

Another episode in my work with Anne confirms that self-disclosure by the analyst can facilitate, rather than impede, a patient's exploration in depth of his or her experience of the treatment relationship. I awoke one morning, bone-tired with a very sore throat, and immediately telephoned Anne, who was my first patient of the day. "I'm sorry for the short notice," I said, "but I'm going to have to cancel our appointment today. It's nothing serious. I think I've got that twenty-four-hour virus that's been going around, so I hope to be in tomorrow." Anne thanked me for calling and wished me a speedy recovery.

Now, it's very rare that I cancel an hour on short notice, and I thought it likely Anne would worry if I didn't explain the reasons for my cancellation. I'm sure some colleagues would argue that by reassuring Anne, I foreclosed a useful opportunity for her to investigate her fantasies about my cancellation—for example, fantasies expressing hostile wishes toward me. My view is very different. I think that had I canceled without explanation, it would have been a contrived and mysterious act, and such unnatural behavior on my part would have afforded Anne little opportunity to investigate her manner of participation in ordinary human relationships.

Anne began our next meeting by reporting a dream from the night following my cancellation. Her dream was that she was lying on a couch, reading a book by Faulkner. Anne's first association to the dream was the title of one of Faulkner's novels, *As I Lay Dying*. That made her remember that after my call, she'd had the idea that maybe I was sicker than I realized. Anne was embarrassed to recall her idea because she felt it reflected her childish anger at me for not keeping our appointment: she was dying to see me, and I should drop dead for canceling!

Clearly, my reassuring self-disclosure did not prevent Anne from entertaining a hostile fantasy toward me. In fact, it seems likely that having had my explanation for canceling the session made it easier for Anne to recognize that imagining me gravely ill was an expression of her own anger. If I had left her in the dark about why I canceled, she could have more easily chalked up her *As I Lay Dying* dream to realistic worries about me.

7

Keeping It Real

One way to understand how clinical psychoanalysis can become impractical is to think of it as losing touch with reality. Traditionally, psychoanalysts have taken the view that a special reality is created by the psychoanalytic encounter—sometimes referred to as "a different level" of reality, a "potential space," or a "unique subjectivity." According to traditional theory, the patient's "internal" or "psychic" reality is the proper subject of clinical investigation, as opposed to considerations of "external" reality, which are set aside for the purposes of analytic work. So, for example, what is often called "reality testing"—when an analyst compares his or her view of the reported facts of a patient's life outside the treatment with the patient's view of them—is traditionally regarded as a misguided departure from psychoanalytic technique. The patient is encouraged to report whatever thoughts come to mind and instructed not to be concerned about how unrealistic they may or may not be. Exploration of the patient's fantasy life, in and of itself, is the essential psychoanalytic project, according to traditional theory.

A practical approach to psychoanalysis, on the other hand, regards treatment as an encounter that takes place within ordinary, everyday reality. The relationship between analyst and patient is no different from any other interpersonal relationship, except that an unusual degree of candor is called for. In fact, it is precisely because the treatment relationship is essentially like any other that the patient has an opportunity, by examining his or her participation in the treatment relationship, to learn about his or her participation in interpersonal relationships generally.

To make a distinction between "internal" and "external" reality is to engage in an intellectual exercise that has no clinical value. In practice, there is no internal and external; there are only constructions of reality—the patient's constructions and the analyst's constructions—in which individual personal psychology and environmental stimuli are inextricable. Practical analytic treatment is organized toward the goal of changing the patient's constructions of reality so as to achieve less distress and more satisfaction for the patient, which translates into alteration of specific behaviors and attitudes; and this is accomplished, in no small part, by the analyst offering novel views of reality that the patient can compare and contrast with his or her own familiar ones. Thus, reality testing, rather than being avoided as an interference with exploration of the patient's psychic life, is at the heart of a practical psychoanalytic treatment process.

Here is a clinical report that highlights the importance of being concerned with judgments about reality in practical psychoanalysis and illustrates the role of reality testing in work with a patient.

MARGARET

Margaret was a thirty-year-old accountant in treatment because of suicidally severe depression. Concerned about her condition, I was meeting with her four times a week at the time the following sequence of events took place.

It was the day before Passover. Margaret, who was Jewish, was feeling terrible about having to be all by herself for the holiday. She had been invited to a friend's Seder, but she was going to cancel out because she'd gotten a cold and didn't want to risk giving it to her friend and her friend's family. In all Margaret's previous descriptions, the friend had sounded to me like a happy-go-lucky type, besides which the friend had two small children, one in preschool and one in grade school, so that full exposure to the San Francisco Bay Area viral pool was likely a fait accompli. It seemed to me reasonable that rather than opt for self-abnegation all on her own, Margaret might at least explain the situation to her friend and hear what the friend had to say.

Margaret and I had been talking for a while in analysis about her tendency to regard herself as an obnoxious person and her deep fear that nobody really wanted to have her around. This idea about herself appeared to have originated, at least in part, from Margaret's sense that her mother, though basically caring and responsible, wasn't ever very interested in Margaret and had found her an imposition much of the time. I had the impression that Margaret's judgment about how to handle the Passover problem was colored by expectations relating to her childhood experience of her mother.

When I explained my point of view to Margaret, she was aghast. She wouldn't dream of putting her friend on the spot by asking her about coming to the Seder with a cold. What I was suggesting seemed selfish and inconsiderate. "Are you partisan on my behalf because I'm your patient?" she wondered, "Or do you just have a basically egoistic world view?" Margaret asserted with some alarm that her attitude about such things seemed very different from mine. She almost canceled her session that day, she told me, except she felt that as a physician, part of the risk I accepted in doing my work was exposure to disease—it came with the territory. Margaret's associations continued on in this vein for a bit.

Eventually, I said that I understood her thinking about coming in, but I added a question: Did Margaret feel that I should cancel appointments when I had gotten a cold or the flu? Because, I told her, I didn't. "Does that seem irresponsible?" I asked. I explained that my attitude was that proximity to people who are ill is part of what we all encounter in stores and restaurants, on airplanes, and elsewhere. "So when I've got a virus, I said, "I may avoid shaking hands and such, but I don't cancel as long as I think I can work effectively." Margaret considered my policy with mixed feelings. She liked the idea of my remaining available to her, but didn't like being put at risk.

Mulling over what I'd said, Margaret arrived at the conclusion that she may have been a bit more cautious than she needed to be. She thought that I was trying to do the right thing, according to my judgment. She knew that some people—responsible and nice people— were less concerned than she about possibly causing one another to catch cold and such. In the course of these reflections, Margaret mentioned that she thought she was phobic, isolated, and depressed like her mother. This was the first time Margaret had described her mother in this light. Previously, she had portrayed her mother as sort of a passionate intellectual, with her nose too buried in a book to pay attention to her daughter. Now we discussed the new image of Margaret's mother and its implications, including Margaret's recognition that she had been trying to make light of her mother's isolation, chalking it up to bookishness, in order to fend off a sense of her mother's capacity for profound withdrawal from the world.

I suggested to Margaret that perhaps feeling phobic, isolated, and depressed like her mother was a state of mind that she actually sought out because it permitted her to feel like her mother, and feeling like her mother was one of the only ways available to Margaret to feel close to her mother. Margaret cried, silently. After a while, she began to talk about her pain and confusion about what had always been her mother's unavailability. Sometimes Margaret thought her mother really loved her, but was just terribly inhibited about expressing it. At other times she thought her mother just didn't want to have anything to do with her. "It's the same with you," Margaret told me. "Even though you seem to be generally interested and involved, I expect that at any time you might get tired of me and tell me that we have to stop treatment."

The next time we met, Margaret began with an account of how she had decided to ask her friend whether it would be all right for her to come to the Seder. Her friend had replied that Margaret must have the same cold that her kids already had, not to worry at all! Margaret felt relieved and a little silly. She had a great time with her friend and her friend's family on Passover. Margaret described the events of her visit in great detail. She was aware of feeling grateful to me and of wanting to thank me by describing how much fun it had been for her to feel like she belonged somewhere on the holiday. She was really glad that I had questioned her assumption that she couldn't go, and also that I hadn't insisted that she adopt my point of view.

Later, Margaret got back to thinking about the unpredictable distance she felt from her mother growing up. It had been as if her mother considered being emotionally engaged a burden—the need to have strong feelings threatened and upset her. Margaret recalled that once when she was about eight years old, she lacerated her scalp in a playground accident. The injury turned out to be quite minor, but when it happened there was immediately a great deal of bleeding and it was very scary. Margaret had run home and found her mother, who, as soon as she saw Margaret, began yelling at her angrily for having injured herself.

The threat of an irritable outburst from her mother was always in her mind, Margaret felt, but her more predominant, and in some ways more hurtful, experience had been of being out of contact with her mother and left on her own. Especially, she had no sense of a connection with her mother around feminine things—how to shop, how to dress, how to flirt, how to behave and value herself as a woman—and as a result she had developed into a socially uncomfortable tomboy.

Eventually, Margaret's father came into her thoughts. She talked about having been conscious throughout her childhood of depending on him for attention and warmth. If something troubled her, she went to her father rather than her mother. If she had a fight with her parents, it was her father who would reach out to her to make it up. Of course, he couldn't really help her with the female stuff. As a child, Margaret remembered, she often wished she were a boy so that she could be closer to her father. Puberty increased her discomfort. She was a funny-looking misfit with hair sticking out in all directions, whose clothes never looked right. Margaret was quite teary as she talked about how unhappy she was growing up. When her father was pleased with her, it helped her feel better about herself. I reminded her of her father in a way, Margaret said, when I seem to believe that she is worthwhile and could expect people to like her. The session ended on that note.

The following session began with Margaret's report of a dream: she was in a field bounded by a fence on all four sides. In the field was a huge, powerful bull. Margaret was in the field with the bull, very frightened that the bull was going to attack her. She associated immediately to her analysis and worrying that I might overpower her. The four fenced-in sides of the field were like her four hours every week. Sometimes she felt trapped in here with me. If my voice seemed to be coming from closer, so that she had the impression I was leaning forward, she had the idea I might pounce on her.

I asked Margaret what she thought had happened to make her particularly concerned about me in that way. She said it was probably what she was talking about when she was with me the day before, how dependent on me she'd been getting, as she used to be on her father. It made her feel vulnerable. On one hand, it really made her feel good to think that she might be okay, that maybe she could fit in with people; but on the other hand she knew I could become too important to her. She didn't want to go around terrified of losing me; she didn't want to worry all the time about whether I liked her.

That's how it had been for her with her father, Margaret explained, and it had been especially difficult for her because her father had been pretty self-centered. He always had to be right, to be the big authority. He would hold forth endlessly about something that interested him, and he would get upset if she disagreed with him at all. He was very competitive too. They used to play tennis a lot together, which she loved, but he always had to win. If he started to lose, he could get almost vicious, smashing the ball at her. It reminded her of the bull in the dream.

She knew, too, that there was something exciting about the bull, and that the dream had to do with her confusion about sex. Margaret began to think over how she'd been able to enjoy sex with men at times, but there was always some kind of anxiety lurking, something about getting hurt. Then her father's need to be superior came to mind again.

Margaret continued to think about how she'd always regarded herself as out of it, not knowing how to be a woman. She felt inferior to other women in that way, and isolated from them. Partly, it was that she had never bonded with her mother, wasn't sure at all how her mother saw herself as a woman; partly, it was that her father needed for her to be submissive and give him his way, which was what her mother did. Margaret always knew she didn't want to relate to men the way her mother related to her father, but she didn't know what else to do. She wanted to find out how other girls related to boys, but she could never get close enough to them to find out. She remembered three very popular girls who always hung out together, whom she knew from being on the tennis team with them in high school. They teased her, calling her stuck-up, when she was really only shy.

As I listened to Margaret describing various interchanges with these three girls, my thoughts went to how often Margaret anticipated incorrectly that she would be unwelcome, was unnecessarily self-critical and pessimistic in her interpretation of social interactions, and underestimated people's interest in her. I wondered whether something of the sort might have been happening with her teammates. I explained my thinking to her, asking if perhaps those girls might have teased her in an effort to make contact with her and get to know her better.

Unexpectedly, Margaret flared up in anger at me. She knew they didn't like her, she asserted. They never invited her to do anything. Margaret went on to present a great deal of very convincing evidence that the possibility I had inquired about was very unlikely. She charged me with being just like her father, attached to my own ideas, unable to respect her point of view, needing to be right. "Really?" I said, "I thought I was only asking. I didn't think I was insisting on being right. Actually, I consider you the expert on your childhood, not me."

"That's a lie," Margaret responded. "All of our work together has been based on the premise that I'm not the expert on my childhood." She reminded me that I had often questioned her way of looking at her past, and very usefully too. I acknowledged to Margaret that she was right, of course. In my eagerness to assure her that I was not being a competitive bully like her father, I overstated the case. "Yes," Margaret replied, "I know that. But what you need to think about is why you overreacted." "Well, I thought I answered that," I responded, "I didn't want you to think I was being like your father when I felt I had a very different intention in mind." "Obviously," Margaret commented sarcastically, but didn't pursue it any further. She fell silent, complaining that she didn't really feel like talking to me. After a bit, I picked up on Margaret's use of the word "really," and suggested that maybe she didn't feel like talking to me because she didn't feel like she could say what she really thought about me.

Margaret hesitated for a while longer, then said with obvious trepidation, "This is what I really think about you. You do believe it's important for an analyst to be open and non-authoritarian and you try to be that way with me. It's very helpful. But besides that, I think you have a personal stake in not being seen as domineering and unfair, so that when I see you that way—rightly or wrongly—you're quick to react and to try to sort it out; and that gets in the way of you being able to listen to me sometimes. So, in a way you can wind up doing the very thing you're trying to avoid." "Huh," I grunted, somewhat taken aback. "That's very interesting and a little embarrassing," I said to Margaret. "I never thought of it that way. Those are certainly my sentiments. I'll try to watch to make sure they don't get in the way. I hope you'll tell me if you think that's happening."

"That would be good," Margaret said. Then she added that the funny thing was that she knew I wasn't really unable to listen to her about those girls. Sometimes I could get a little too interested in making my point, but not that time. She knew that I was basically a nice guy. Even if I was a little narcissistic, I was also considerate and caring. She knew she liked me a lot, and she wasn't sure why right then she wanted to pick a fight with me. There was something else going on. It made her nervous to be alone in the room with me, feeling like I was a nice guy and she liked me. She knew it was about sex, somehow.

There were two points at which I very explicitly engaged in reality testing with Margaret, in the sense that I challenged her view of reality. The first time was when I suggested to Margaret that she was wrong to assume that it would be destructively selfish of her to go to dinner at her friend's house with a cold and that her friend wouldn't want her to come; and the second time was when I questioned Margaret's experience of being rejected by her high school teammates. The first time, Margaret eventually came to agree with the alternative view of reality that I proposed, which was quite helpful to her because it allowed her to become aware of her undue caution in general and in particular to have a happy holiday experience. The second time, Margaret disagreed with my alternative view of reality and persuaded me that I was wrong, which was also helpful to her because in the process she brought up an important critical perception of me that she had been entertaining and pursued its implications.

Neither time did Margaret need to defer to me when I questioned the way she constructed reality. She felt free to question me in turn; she made contrary proposals; she obtained further information when she needed it; and she ultimately decided, according to her own lights, what she believed reality to be. On both occasions, reality testing eventuated in the discovery of significant, previously unexamined aspects of Margaret's psychology. First, Margaret's recognition that her customary fearfulness and inhibition had the effect of isolating her from people led her to realize that she was trying to feel close to her mother by being like her mother, at great cost to herself. Then, Margaret's perception of me as being like her father in certain ways, but not in others, led her to become aware that she was made anxious by sexual feelings toward me, as she had been made anxious in the past by sexual feelings toward him.

This episode in Margaret's treatment illustrates that focus on the reality of a patient's daily life and concern with reality testing by no means steer analyst and patient away from exploring the patient's psychology in depth. On the contrary, reality testing points the way to exploration in depth. It also directs exploration in depth toward matters of consequence to the way the patient lives outside the treatment, preventing clinical psychoanalysis from becoming a rarified exercise without therapeutic benefit. Nor does concern with reality and reality testing impede examination of transferences occurring within the analytic treatment relationship; what it does is make it possible for the patient to expose and look into his or her sincerest convictions about *who the analyst really is*, and it is only when that can happen that a patient effectively evaluates how much his or her present experience of the analyst is being affected by legacies from the past. Otherwise, conclusions about transference remain essentially intellectual and hypothetical—which is why, so often, a patient treated in the classical manner requires a second analysis to explore what he or she *really* thought about his or her first analyst (and a third analysis to explore what he or she *really* thought about the second analyst, etc., etc.).

8

The Perils of Neutrality

Analysts have given themselves and their patients a good deal of trouble over the years by trying to remain neutral when conducting psychoanalytic treatments. The concept of *analytic neutrality* is well intended. It represents an attempt to safeguard patients from being unduly influenced by their analysts. It goes without saying that analysts want patients to be free to choose their own ways of feeling better. The problem is that an analyst trying to practice analytic neutrality doesn't protect the patient's autonomy—and it gets in the way of helping the patient.

Freud was especially concerned with the problem of untoward influence because he was at pains to distinguish clinical psychoanalysis from hypnotic suggestion and related treatment methods that achieve therapeutic results at the expense of the patient's self-determination. Accordingly, he recommended that analysts adopt a stance of *indifferenz* (literally, indifference) when performing their clinical activities. *Indifferenz*, which came to be translated as *analytic neutrality*, has two aspects: the first is impartiality on the analyst's part with regard to the patient's conflicts, and the second is the analyst remaining, as far as possible, emotionally uninvolved in analytic work.

Now, there are certainly some conflicts with which a patient may struggle concerning which an analyst has no business taking sides. In these instances, impartiality is not a matter of analytic technique; it is simply the result of common sense and lack of presumption on the analyst's part. For example, when Ralph (see Chapter 2) was deciding whether to pursue his dream and study guitar, even though it would mean exposing his family to risk, I didn't feel in any position to have an opinion about what he ought to do. On the other hand, there are conflicts with which a patient struggles concerning which it can make good sense for an analyst to take sides. For example, when Margaret (see Chapter 7) was wondering whether to give herself the pleasure of attending her friend's Seder, I thought she should attend and I told her so. Again, the determining factor was my personal judgment that Margaret's self-deprivation was unnecessary; analytic theory had nothing to do with it.

Sometimes it is useful for an analyst to be partisan concerning a patient's conflict and sometimes it isn't. There are no technical rules for deciding which is true in any given instance. The principle of analytic neutrality directs an analyst *always* to avoid being partisan, and that renders an analyst who practices analytic neutrality ineffective. Witness the famous quip by a patient: "I'm going to look for an analyst with only one arm, so he can't always say, 'Well on the one hand . . . but on the other hand . . .'" Of course, traditional analysts violate the principle of analytic neutrality all the time when they try to help their patients, but they do so reluctantly and less frequently than would be optimal. And when practitioners of analytic neutrality do communicate personal opinions to their patients, since they can't square what they are doing with their theory they tend to communicate indirectly and disavow the participation of their personal opinions. An atmosphere of hypocrisy is created that does the treatment no good at all.

Also, it's impossible for an analyst who is responsibly engaged in treatment not to be emotionally involved, and the analyst's emotional involvement invariably comes through to the patient. All that happens when an analyst aspires to a position of analytic neutrality is that the analyst feels guilty about his or her emotional involvement, tries to deny it, and tries to hide it. The resulting stress and constraint necessarily get in the way of an authentic and productive treatment relationship. This is especially unfortunate, inasmuch as there is no reason to believe that an analyst expressing his or her feelings to a patient is, in and of itself, problematic.

Consider the following report of how I took sides in a patient's conflicts, how my emotional involvement was communicated to the patient, and what the consequences were.

DIANE

Diane, a cardiologist in her early thirties, had serious problems at work. Despite having done well in her residency and fellowship, she was aware of a lack of self-confidence that held her back. She turned down opportunities for advancement because she was afraid of failing. In particular, she avoided situations in which she would have to collaborate closely with others; she was very pessimistic about being able to get on with her colleagues. She sometimes flew off the handle or, more often, she sullenly withdrew when she was angry. Diane felt in general that she was not a likable person, and worried that no one wanted to be friends with her.

Much of Diane's self-condemnation had to do with her guilty sense that she had always been envious and hostile, going back to her resentment of her two-year-older sister. At six years of age, the sister had been diagnosed with juvenile diabetes, which proved extremely difficult to control. The sister had been the focal point of Diane's parents' anxious concern, ever since Diane could remember. At school, Diane's sister was a mediocre student, which increased the distress of the parents, both of whom were university professors. Diane, who had always done quite well academically, felt neglected. Her parents rarely praised her good grades; they were too preoccupied with her sister's poor performance.

When Diane told me how it had been for her as a child, I commented that while I could understand that her family situation had been very difficult, it wasn't clear to me why her main reaction had been to envy and resent her sister, given the painful problem that had been the reason for her sister receiving attention and given the unpleasant kind of attention her sister received. Diane explained how she recalled wishing her sister would die and feeling awful about it. Over several weeks, she elaborated her guilty view of her sibling rivalry. Without discrediting the sincerity of Diane's feelings, I continued to question her focus on her sister as the cause of her childhood distress. I asked Diane if her parents had acknowledged that their preoccupation with Diane's sister had left Diane shortchanged. Had they noted her upset? Had they tried to help her with it?

Clearly, my questions indicated my skepticism about the emphasis Diane placed on her envy, hostility, and guilt toward her sister. I was wondering whether Diane's hostility toward her sister and her guilt about it might have the important defensive function of sparing Diane from experiencing serious criticisms of her parents and accompanying awful feelings. I explicitly stated to Diane both my judgments about the situation in her family during her childhood, as she described it, and the hypothesis that I was entertaining as a result.

Diane saw the sense in my perspective and she considered it, but she had mixed feelings about it. She was troubled that she might be painting a self-servingly distorted picture of events to which I was responding. In this connection, one terrible memory stood out in her mind. When her sister was twelve and Diane ten, the girls were left alone without a babysitter while their parents took an overnight business trip to a city an hour's plane flight away. That evening, Diane's sister began to complain that she didn't feel well, and got suddenly very spacey and uncommunicative. Alarmed, Diane called her parents at their hotel, but they were out. She tried to contact neighbors. Unfortunately, it was Saturday night and no one was home. Her sister became dead-white and sweaty. Her eyes were closed and Diane couldn't wake her up. Desperate, Diane called 911. The paramedics who responded to the call and the doctors at the hospital to which her sister was taken told Diane that her sister had just missed dying, apparently the result of a mistake she had made in giving herself her insulin injection. That night was traumatic for Diane. Ever since, she had been tortured by recalling how her sister had looked lying on the floor, and the thought that maybe she, Diane, had made it all happen because she wanted her sister to die. Why hadn't she realized the nature of her sister's difficulty and given her sister some orange juice and sugar?

I asked Diane why she charged herself, rather than her parents, with irresponsibility. I said that it seemed to me she had handled the situation at least as well as anyone could expect from a ten-year-old, whereas most people would never think of leaving two such young girls—one with a dangerous medical condition—alone without child care or even anyone they could contact in case of emergency, as her parents had done. Diane had associated to the childhood incident as a dramatic illustration of her hostility and guilt toward her sister, but to me it confirmed how Diane's self-blame arose from her struggle to avoid facing persistent, very disturbing perceptions of her parents.

Diane had a strong reaction to my view of the incident, so different from her own. She felt relief in a way, and could catch glimpses of a more positive self-image that might lift her out of the depression with which she had lived for so long. At the same time, she was aware of an awful, hard-to-define anxiety, a feeling of dread in the pit of her stomach. When I asked her to elaborate on the feeling, she reluctantly reported the thought that I seemed outraged at the way her parents had treated her. She worried that I was getting too involved. Again, she brought up her concern that she had somehow misled me.

I acknowledged to Diane that while what she described her parents doing did seem extremely irresponsible to me, my judgment was based entirely upon her portrait of events. If there was more to what had happened than was apparent to me, then we would hope to find it out. However, at this point it certainly looked as if Diane was trying at all costs to avoid facing some terribly upsetting things about the way she had been brought up. Given what we knew so far, I was certainly outraged on her behalf. What worried her about that?

Diane began to sob uncontrollably. Eventually she was able to try to sort out her feelings. She thought I understood her, and she was deeply moved, but very saddened by that. There was something about how I seemed to be primarily concerned with her welfare and trying to help—even when she questioned my judgment. That made her feel so good; it made her feel terrible, too. A sad recollection, which Diane had not mentioned before, came to mind of what it was like always to come home to an empty apartment. Both her parents taught until early evening every day, and her sister took to staying out with friends all the time once she got to high school. My outrage showed how much I cared about her, how involved I was in trying to help her. Diane went on to describe the sense she had always had of her mother's coldness and her father's preoccupation with his work above everything else. She had never felt from her parents the kind of concern she felt from me. She hated having to face that. What could she do about it now? Her father was dead and her mother was in a nursing home.

About a year later, Diane was discussing sexual problems she was having with a boyfriend. He just wasn't interested, she said. She compared his distant attitude with her mother's. Diane found her relationship with this man wonderful in many ways. They had a lot in common and enjoyed doing things together. But they didn't make love very often and when they did it seemed routine. I didn't think it was obvious what was going on. Considering Diane's history, it seemed possible that without realizing it she might be creating, at least to an extent, what she experienced as her boyfriend's disinterest. For example, was he responding to negative expectations that Diane was communicating to him? Or, if he did have a problem, how actively was Diane trying to address it? I inquired along these lines.

Diane felt criticized and betrayed by me. I had been so sympathetic about her sense of deprivation by her mother. Why was I sticking up for her boyfriend? Was I sexist? Overidentified with him? I said I didn't think so, although, obviously, it was always possible that I was sexist or identified with her boyfriend in some way I wasn't aware of. But what struck me as important, I told her, was that she felt so attacked by me, when clearly my intent—even if misguided—was to help her see if she could find more sexual pleasure within a relationship she valued highly. As we discussed Diane's reaction to my inquiry, she became aware that she was uncomfortable about me encouraging her to explore the possibility of greater sexual activity.

Eventually, what came to light was Diane's adolescent anxiety about her father's appreciation of her emerging femininity. Now Diane revisited her image of her mother as distant, and modified it a bit. It was true that her mother was reserved, and that both her parents were capable of a kind of self-centeredness that hurt their children; but Diane also realized that her guilt about her competitiveness with her mother had caused Diane to underestimate her father's interest in her and overestimate her mother's aloofness.

Though my questions about Diane's sex life initially made her angry, they led to exposure of anxiety on Diane's part about being sexually active and attractive to men, and to a very useful investigation of the origin of those anxieties. Ironically, though, my questions proved to be quite off the point as far as the future of her relationship with her boyfriend was concerned. As it turned out, he eventually confessed to Diane with great regret that he had never really found women sexually exciting, and that he had decided to go public with a homosexual life that he had been keeping secret for years.

Diane was struggling to resolve a conflict and I certainly took sides in her struggle. I consistently stood for her wish to feel good about herself and to enjoy her life, and against what seemed to me to be the excessive, harsh demands of her conscience—expressed in her inhibitions and unrealistic self-criticisms. I made no secret of my partisan position. Furthermore, I had strong feelings about a number of matters related to Diane's problem, which I communicated to her. My participation in our work together was by no means dispassionate. Analytic neutrality means not taking sides in the patient's conflict and not being emotionally involved in the work. I was decidedly not analytically neutral in either sense of the term.

There is nothing unusual about this sequence of events in Diane's treatment. Whenever an analyst is helpful to a patient, it is necessarily by means of exerting a very personal influence, as I did. Insofar as an analyst provides a patient with novel perspectives to consider, those perspectives arise from the analyst's own values and preferences. Insofar as an analyst is able to negotiate corrective emotional experiences with a patient (see Chapter 5), those experiences are not merely intellectual, and the analyst's emotional involvement is an integral part of them. A truly neutral analyst would be, essentially, absent from the treatment.

An analyst might like to believe that by adopting a stance of analytic neutrality the analyst can protect a patient from the analyst's personal influence, but it is not the case. On the contrary, when an analyst believes that he or she is able to practice analytic neutrality, the analyst idealizes and deceives himself or herself and invites the patient to collude. Then, the analyst's personal influence is all the more constraining for being covert. The best safeguard against infringing upon a patient's autonomy is for an analyst to acknowledge the highly personal nature of his or her participation in the treatment, so that the patient feels free to evaluate the analyst's contributions for what they are.

9

The Limits of Self-Awareness

It's troubling for an analyst to realize that when he or she helps a patient it is by exerting a highly personal influence on the patient. It's even more troubling for an analyst to realize that much of the highly personal influence he or she exerts is determined by factors of which the analyst is quite unaware at the time—by the analyst's unconscious desires, assumptions, interests, and the like. Analysts have wanted to believe that they can generally apply an impersonal, objective method to their work, in something of the same way that surgeons or engineers do. The idea has been that an analyst can be aware of a baseline working state in which he or she is relatively free from the intrusion of idiosyncratic psychological motivations, and that the analyst can detect deviations from this baseline state, termed *countertransference reactions*, by noting emotional arousal in himself or herself. Self-analysis on the analyst's part prevents a countertransference reaction from being a problematic intrusion, and awareness of a countertransference reaction can even be made use of as a clue to what is happening in treatment at the moment.

One problem with this wishfully idealized view of the relation between an analyst's personal psychology and his or her technique is that by the time an analyst becomes aware of a countertransference reaction, the reaction has already manifested itself behaviorally and had an influence in the treatment. Awareness *instead of* action is not possible. The philosopher and psychologist William James pointed out that our emotions are actually observations of our actions—we know that we're angry when we feel our muscles tense, our stomachs churn, and so on. Sometimes what an analyst notices about himself or herself that allows the analyst to recognize the existence of countertransference is an action on the very finest scale of magnitude—a subtle kinesthetic tension for example. It may be tempting to believe that such actions go unnoticed by patients, so that for all practical purposes the analyst's awareness of countertransference can precede any behavioral expression of countertransference by the analyst. But experience indicates otherwise. Even the slightest nuance of disposition influences how an analyst hears material, influences whether the analyst decides to intervene or remain silent, influences how the analyst chooses his or her words and the tone in which they are spoken if the analyst does decide to say something—all of which are of the greatest importance to the treatment.

A second and perhaps even more important problem is that an analyst can never become aware of all the personal idiosyncratic factors at play in determining his or her activity. The greatest part of them remains unconscious. For that reason, the concept of *countertransference,* in and of itself, is misleading because it implies that the personal element of an analyst's responses can be identified and separated from an analyst's impersonal, technical functioning, whereas the truth is that the two are inextricable. Every aspect and every moment of an analyst's activity is thoroughly saturated by what has been called countertransference. Therefore, it is dangerously misguided for an analyst to think that he or she can identify a baseline state of relative detachment in which countertransference plays a minimal role. Psychoanalysts should be the first to recognize that one's conscious awareness of emotional involvement is in no way an indicator of one's actual emotional involvement. For example . . .

ETHAN

Ethan was a thirty-one-year-old emergency room physician, the son of an eminent surgeon. Ethan had always been certain that he could never equal his father's achievements. When his father died, Ethan began to feel that his own life had no meaning. He found himself avoiding people. It became harder and harder to get out of bed in the morning and go to work. After six months of this, he sought treatment. Ethan knew about psychoanalysis. He considered it the most rigorous form of psychotherapy. Since Ethan always held himself to the highest standard, he asked to be seen four times a week and to use the couch.

Ethan began his analysis by investigating the exaggerated admiration he had always felt for his father, as well as his need to engage in a hopeless competition with his father. Ethan thought about what he experienced as his mother's covert resentment of her husband, covered over by her public adulation of him. Looking back on his childhood, Ethan realized that he felt his mother recruited him to be her champion against his father—a task to which Ethan felt woefully inadequate. He connected feeling thrust into this difficult position in the family with troubling inhibitions and self doubts from which he had suffered for a long time, even before his father's death. Ethan began to feel a lot better. He became excited about his future.

I had the impression that Ethan regarded me essentially as an ideal parent: omnipotent, like his father, but encouraging and accepting instead of being distant and critical the way his father was; attentive and engaged, like his mother, but not communicating the kinds of exploitive demands that she had. I assumed that Ethan would eventually take note of my clay feet, in detail; but in the meantime I was pleased by all the good things that were happening in the treatment and I was enjoying our honeymoon as much as Ethan was.

The session on which I want to focus began with Ethan talking about an experience he had earlier in the day that was still very much with him. A young woman was brought to the emergency room comatose, on the verge of death, and Ethan spent several hours struggling to save her. He determined that the patient was in hypothyroid crisis, and he was able to stabilize her. By the time Ethan's shift was over, the patient had been admitted to the hospital with a reasonably optimistic prognosis. Ethan described the anxiety he felt when the patient first arrived, his concern that he might not make the right diagnosis, that he might not manage the treatment properly, and his relief when the patient's condition began to improve. He pursued his thoughts along those lines.

I asked a few clarifying questions, but was generally silent. I was aware of listening to Ethan's account with interest. I was impressed with his conscientiousness and his quietly passionate devotion to his work. Furthermore, from what I knew, hypothyroid crisis was not at all an easy diagnosis to make, so that Ethan had every reason to be quite proud of himself for having saved the patient's life. If this sense of accomplishment did not occur to him, I planned to inquire why it hadn't made an appearance.

Given my state of mind, I was quite surprised when Ethan suddenly interrupted his account to remark that he felt as if he had lost my attention, that my thoughts were elsewhere. Having voiced this idea, he dismissed it as foolish and turned back to reflecting upon his experience in the emergency room. After a while, when it was clear that Ethan wasn't going to come back on his own initiative to his potentially critical comment about me, I pointed out his willingness to let it drop. He said he didn't know why he thought that my attention had lapsed; he knew that I was listening. I replied that apparently he wasn't so sure, at least for a moment. Could he recall what led him to the thought that he'd lost my attention? Ethan drew a blank. I encouraged him to say whatever came to mind, even if it seemed irrelevant, but we didn't get anywhere; nor did it prove productive when I pointed out to Ethan that his idea about me must have arisen for some reason and invited him to associate specifically to the image of me with my thoughts elsewhere.

Eventually, I told Ethan that my own experience was that I had been quite involved in listening to what he was saying. I added that, in fact, I was aware of feeling particularly interested in what seemed to me to be his reluctance to express pride in having made a difficult and crucial diagnosis. Given my view of what was going on for me, I explained, my speculation about Ethan's thought that he had lost my attention was that it might have been prompted by the idea that I would find it hard to hear about his success.

This suggestion made sense to Ethan. He thought about the possibility that I might feel bad about not being a "real doctor." He recalled that a few moments ago my voice seemed to be coming from afar, as if I had turned away. It was a characteristic gesture of his father's, when his father was uninterested or impatient with what someone was saying, to turn his head and gaze into space. Ethan went on to reflect upon his father's need always to be the surgeon in charge. He was a loving and kind man, really, but he had to be the authority. Ethan wondered if maybe I was a bit like his father in that way, though he hadn't really seen it. "You seem to want me to be all I can be," Ethan said to me. "But after all, you're human. You might be competitive with me, even if it isn't obvious."

Listening to Ethan's response to my intervention, I wondered, of course, to what extent he was telling me what he thought I wanted to hear, compliantly confirming my hypothesis that he was having difficulty telling me about his success. It seemed to me that he moved pretty quickly from talking about my vulnerability to talking about his father. The thoughts about his father seem spontaneous and relevant, but it was as if Ethan was hastening to establish that his idea that I might be envious of him for being a real doctor was unrealistic—just a transference fantasy. On the other hand, for Ethan to even entertain the idea that I might feel inferior to him was uncharacteristic. It was a lively, here-and-now thought that was very much at odds with his usual idealization of me. Though he only stayed briefly with his unflattering view of me, he did get back to it when he conjectured about the possibility that I might have been covertly competitive with him.

These assessments, back and forth, all went on in my mind while I was listening to Ethan, and in a much shorter time than it takes to report them. Also, something else occurred to me. When Ethan brought up the image of my turning my head away, I immediately recalled, earlier in the hour, speaking and looking off to my left, away from Ethan. I had been trying to see if the signal light on my phone was blinking to indicate that a new voice mail had been received. I'd been waiting to hear from a friend whom I was meeting later for dinner about whether he'd been able to get us into a new restaurant I'd been wanting to try. As I remembered this moment from before, I felt hungry. I recognized that Ethan was right: my attention had been elsewhere for an instant and he had picked up on it, cued by a change in the direction from which my voice seemed to be coming when I spoke to him.

Moreover, I had to ask myself why I had thought to check my phone at that particular moment, why I had forgotten about the momentary distraction during my subsequent efforts to investigate with Ethan his idea about my thoughts having been elsewhere, and why I got hungry when I eventually recalled the incident. My first thought was that I wanted to eat to keep from being depressed, something I used to do all the time as a child when my mother was ill. I thought of Ethan working to save his patient's life, and I realized that all the while I had been listening to him and imagining what had gone on in the emergency room, I had been picturing the woman, Ethan's patient, in the image of my mother. I imagined the patient the way my mother had looked during her eventually fatal chronic illness—overweight and not unlike a patient in hypothyroid crisis I had happened to see during my internship. I couldn't save my mother. The severely hypothyroid woman I saw during my internship had not been my patient; I hadn't gotten a chance to save her. Was Ethan right that I felt inferior to him because he was a real doctor who could save patients' lives? In a way. But one of the reasons I became a psychiatrist was that in my mother's case it had been her psychological response to her illness, rather than the physical illness per se, that had been her ruin; so I felt that in my way I was saving lives as I wished I could have saved hers.

Meanwhile, Ethan had gotten back to familiar territory. He was thinking about how much he had always wanted his father's good opinion and how he had probably overestimated his father's criticism of him because he had felt guilty about allying with his mother. When Ethan reached a natural pause, I told him that I had realized that he had been right about my being distracted: I remembered that I had wanted to check whether a call I was expecting had come in, and I had turned to look while asking him a question. Apparently, he had noticed. Ethan's first thought in response to my admission was that he wondered if the call had to do with something I was worried about. Then he chuckled. I didn't really sound worried, he observed. Probably he thought about something bad happening to me, he mused, because he was pissed off about my attention having been taken away from him. I explained the nature of the phone call I was expecting, acknowledging that Ethan's perception of my attention having been elsewhere in that moment had been correct, and I apologized.

Ethan got teary. He was obviously enormously touched and pleased. "This is great," he said. "It's no big deal that your mind wandered for a minute—that's got to happen from time to time. What's a big deal to me," Ethan went on, "is that we can talk like this. You can admit when you've made a mistake, when I show you something you didn't know. I don't have to walk on eggs around you, worrying what's going to happen if you feel challenged. I wish I'd had this with my dad. I wonder how much of the problem between us was him and his need to be the big shot, and how much was me and my guilt about playing up to my mom."

The first thirty minutes or so of my meeting with Ethan were typical of an analyst's daily routine. I was aware of being calm, interested, and felt that I was thoughtfully listening to my patient in the context of a treatment that was going well. There seemed little reason to believe that my view of things was being especially influenced by idiosyncratic personal reactions. But if we look closely, we can see that my listening to Ethan was shaped at every step of the way by my own history, my theoretical preferences, and my individual psychology.

As Ethan told his story of the day's events, I began to consider that he might be inhibited about being proud of himself. I took that particular focus, at least in part, because of a memory of mine from internship days that hypothyroid crisis is a difficult diagnosis to make, and because I happened to have seen what it took to save the life of a patient in hypothyroid crisis. Another analyst with a different personal history might have listened quite differently. For example, some analysts would certainly have heard in what Ethan was saying references to his experience of the treatment relationship. Ethan's narrative, depicting the drama of a doctor's successful rescue of his difficult patient, could easily have been construed as an expression of Ethan's passive wishes, a fantasy of being repaired and saved by his analyst. Now, I happen to be skeptical of the assumption that everything a patient says in treatment alludes in some way to his or her analyst; I consider that a self-referential attitude on the analyst's part invites the patient to be preoccupied with the treatment relationship and becomes a self-fulfilling prophecy. But we all choose our preferred theories, as we know very well, for reasons that have everything to do with our individual characters. These are just a couple of examples of personal factors that influenced the way I heard what Ethan said— factors of which I was *aware* while I was listening to him.

The way things developed, I had the opportunity to recognize retrospectively that important factors of which I had been quite *un-aware* had also been in operation. Because Ethan confronted me with my lapse of attention, I realized that as I was listening to Ethan's emergency room story, my sadness at my mother's illness and death, my urges to rescue her, my rivalry with other rescuers, and a host of longstanding wishes, conflicts, and anxieties had been stirred up. I had not been conscious of any of these concerns. Nonetheless, they had exerted a decisive influence upon how I understood what Ethan was saying.

My session with Ethan revealed to me with unusual vividness the limitations of my self-awareness. But there was nothing unusual about the limitations themselves. An analyst's perceptions are constantly influenced by a variety of conscious and unconscious idiosyncratic factors, and the analyst can never know, at any given moment, to what degree or entirely in what manner his or her listening is being shaped by highly personal thoughts and feelings of which he or she is unaware. Any useful conception of analytic technique has to take this condition into account.

10

Acting Out and Enactment

Acting out is a clinical concept that was formulated by Freud over a hundred years ago. That it is still widely used by psychoanalysts to direct their clinical work testifies to the inertia that has impeded progress in psychoanalysis, since the concept of acting out is based upon a model of the mind that has long since been rendered obsolete.

It was Freud's idea that the nervous system is a network of circuits through which currents flow hydraulically—currents could be blocked, dammed up, reverse direction, and so on; and Freud believed that psychic impulses, being manifestations of activity in the nervous system, could be conceptualized in the same way. Therefore, Freud thought, a psychic impulse can flow in one direction and result in motor action, in which case no mental activity will take place; or, if the pathway to motor action is blocked, the impulse can flow in an opposite direction and stimulate the sensory apparatus from within, giving rise to mental activity. For instance, Freud reasoned that dreaming, a mental activity, happens because sleep paralysis makes motor action impossible. According to Freud's model of the mind, thought and action are mutually exclusive alternatives, related to one another in a zero–sum system: the more action, the less thought, and vice versa.

Freud concluded that since clinical psychoanalysis depends upon the patient's psychic impulses manifesting themselves in thought, acting out of the patient's impulses has to be prevented in order for treatment to succeed. Therefore, for example, Freud originally required his patients to suspend all sexual activity, so that their sexual urges could become available for analysis in the form of fantasies. Of course, the treatments that Freud conducted were very brief. As psychoanalytic treatments began to last longer and longer, the injunction against sexual activity was abandoned (an analyst who insisted upon it would have a very small practice, indeed!), but only for reasons of convenience, not because the underlying theory changed. Even today, traditional analysts are reluctant to answer their patients' questions, believing that if a patient's wish to know is acted out by having his or her question answered, the wish will not manifest itself fully in thought and therefore will not be available for analysis.

Freud's model of the mind was consistent with the neurological science of his day. However, for a very long while we have known that neural circuits do not work by having currents flow hydraulically through them. In the nervous system, there is no damming up or reversing the direction of impulses. Therefore, the entire basis for the concept of acting out is erroneous. There is no reason to conceptualize thought and action as mutually exclusive alternatives; in fact, thought is best understood as trial action. Nonetheless, despite the model of the mind upon which it is based having been invalidated, the concept of acting out endures in psychoanalysis.

About twenty years ago, the term *enactment* started to appear in the psychoanalytic literature. An enactment is an interaction between analyst and patient in which the unconscious motivations of one or the other are expressed—an interaction in which an unconscious fantasy of the analyst's or of the patient's is realized. Enactment is regarded as something that an analyst should try to avoid. However, it is also understood that, analysts being fallible, enactments are bound to occur. When an enactment does occur, damage control can be instituted and the enactment put to some use after the fact, if it is identified and examined. This view of enactment involves the very same thinking that has always applied to acting out. Essentially, *enactment* is a euphemism for *acting out*. The older term *acting out* is directly linked to Freud's early, obsolete model of the mind. The newer term *enactment* leaves behind that embarrassing theoretical connection; therefore, analysts are more comfortable with it. But there is no substantive difference between the concepts of acting out and enactment, and their implications for technique are the same.

The problem with using the concept of enactment to guide analytic technique is that it assumes that certain interactions between analyst and patient, enactments, express the unconscious motivations of one or the other of the participants, realize their unconscious fantasies, while other interactions between analyst and patient do *not* express the unconscious motivations of one or another of the participants, do *not* realize their unconscious fantasies, or do so to a lesser degree. That assumption is mistaken and misleading. The truth is that *every* interaction between analyst and patient expresses the unconscious motivations of, realizes some unconscious fantasy or other of, *both* participants. For an analyst to think otherwise is naive and will lead the analyst to underestimate his or her personal participation in clinical work.

The concept of enactment is only valid if it is used to denote not *particular* events that *sometimes* occur in treatment, but a *constant* dimension of *all* treatment events. When analyst and patient are able to understand at a moment in treatment how certain of their unconscious motivations have been expressed through their interaction, they identify only a tiny fraction of what goes on continuously but remains for the most part unrecognized. Enactment cannot be minimized, let alone eliminated, from analytic treatment. Nor is enactment an obstacle to analytic work; it is an aspect of productive interactions between patient and analyst as well as unproductive ones.

In discussing Ethan's treatment (see Chapter 9), I gave, in effect, an illustration of how enactment is always a dimension of the analyst's listening, even at unremarkable moments. Now I would like to turn my attention to the analyst's interventions. Good technique is not distinguishable from bad technique according to whether the analyst participates in enactment. An analyst participates in enactment whatever he or she does, when making a useful intervention or when making a terrible mistake. And sometimes the two coincide!

ALAN

Alan came to see me when he was in his late twenties. For years, he had been terribly hemmed in by a host of obsessions, compulsive rituals, and intrusive nonsense thoughts. "Carrara Ferrari, let's take a safari!" he would shout suddenly. Before sitting down, he had to touch each arm of the chair an equal number of times. He had tics and twitches of all kinds. Alan had been diagnosed with Tourette's syndrome and tried on large doses of the medications used to control that condition, but to little effect.

I had the impression that some sort of desperation underlay Alan's frantic preoccupations. They seemed to me to be motivated, rather than being arbitrary neurological outbursts. I explained to Alan that I thought he was terrified of certain thoughts that were coming to his mind and that he was trying to avoid them at all costs by directing his attention toward anything else that occurred to him. I encouraged him to face the threatening thoughts because that was the only way he could get better. I promised him that I would help him deal with whatever came up.

Gradually, Alan began to be aware of violently sadistic fantasies that would come to his mind unbidden and terrify him. In Alan's fantasies, his victims were always women. This outwardly timid and inhibited man was boiling with rage inside. The terrifying fantasies were often prompted by apparently trivial events. A female coworker would close a window that Alan had opened and he would imagine throwing her to the floor and grinding his heel into her face.

As he became able to tolerate these threatening thoughts, Alan's tics, twitches, obsessions, and compulsions went away. It was a miracle cure that thrilled us both. But now we had a new problem to deal with that interfered with Alan's life almost as much as his original symptoms had. Alan couldn't stop ruminating about doing terrible things to women.

The question we needed to answer was: Why was Alan so prone to fury at women? And here we were stuck. Alan had some grievances toward his mother, which we looked into, but none of them seemed very significant. He had a dream in which he was swimming around in a pond, urinating. His urine killed some young corn that was growing on the bottom of the pond. The dream made quite an impression on Alan. He interpreted it as portraying hostility toward a younger sibling in utero. Alan ransacked his mind with characteristic obsessive thoroughness, exploring his feelings toward his six-year-younger sister, trying to dredge up memories of how he felt about her birth, of his reactions to his mother's pregnancy. It all yielded very little.

Alan had trouble sleeping and from time to time he made use of a mild sedative that he got from his internist. When Alan first reported that he was taking the pills, I commented that it would be useful if we could understand the anxiety that was causing his insomnia. Alan decided that it would be better for his treatment if he tried to analyze his bedtime discomfort, rather than trying to medicate it away. He began to reduce his sedative use, and he looked to me for more approval than he felt I was expressing. I commented that not taking the pills seemed to be something Alan felt he was doing at least as much for me as for himself.

One day, Alan came in and announced that he had not taken any sleeping pills for a month. I did not congratulate him and Alan complained about my lack of appreciation for his efforts. "It's like being weaned from the breast," he moaned. "You don't realize how difficult it is." I said, "It's as if you feel like the only person who was ever weaned from the breast." While the content of my remark was perfectly in order, calling Alan's attention to an unrealistic sense of his own uniqueness and of the injustice of his life, there was an edge to the way I put it that Alan certainly felt. The edge came from an unwarranted resentment on my part. After a wonderful beginning, treatment was bogged down and I was very disappointed about not being able to continue my miraculous success. I was getting impatient with

Alan's hyperintellectual style and his whiny complaints. When Alan asserted that I couldn't possibly know the trouble he felt, my reaction was to review some of the more difficult periods in my own past and to ask myself who this guy thought he was, telling *me* about suffering.

Alan blinked and paused fractionally, obviously affected by the hostility he sensed in me, but he didn't comment on it; and I, wanting to deny sentiments that I was not very proud of having communicated to my patient, didn't bring it up either. In fact, I didn't even admit to myself at that moment what I had been feeling when I made my remark. The tone I took with Alan and my denial of it afterward were unjustifiable. The *enactment* aspect of the interaction couldn't have been more conspicuous. What was surprising, and interesting, was how well it turned out!

Instead of reacting explicitly to my tone, Alan took my observation at face value and went on to think compliantly about how what I had said was true. He was not unique in having been weaned from the breast. He had even seen his baby son go through the process not long ago. Alan tried to suppress his upset, but it broke through in the form of a slip of the tongue. He referred to his son as Gary. That was not his son's name. I asked Alan who Gary was. He claimed to know no one named Gary. I suggested to Alan that the name couldn't have come from nowhere and that he seemed reluctant to let his thoughts go freely in association with it. "No," Alan replied, "the only Gary I can think of is the younger brother my parents told me about that was stillborn when I was eighteen months old." (!) Alan was sure he had mentioned this part of his history before. Initially, he seemed to have no awareness of what a dramatically significant omission it was that during all the time he had been meticulously searching his memory for experiences concerning his mother's pregnancy with a younger sibling, Gary had never come to mind. When I pointed this out to Alan, he was shocked. Over the next while, he began to recount a chapter of his early life that he had completely avoided thinking about before in his treatment.

After the delivery of his stillborn brother, Alan's mother had suffered a severe postpartum depression. A dream depicted what Alan's childhood understanding of his mother's depression must have been.

In the dream, his mother was squatting and had a miserable, dejected expression. Something was terribly wrong. A long lip of bleeding flesh drooped from between her legs. Alan felt a strong urge to go toward her to help, but at the same time he dreaded touching her. The dream indicated that fantasies about the stillbirth, about his mother's genitalia, and about the loss of body products by excretion all had become confused and condensed in Alan's mind into an impression that his mother was depressed because she had lost something important. This impression resulted in a conflict between Alan's wish to substitute himself for what his mother was missing in order to cure her depression and make her once more loving and lovable, and his fear of having to sacrifice himself to restore her loss. In fact, though we hadn't realized it, this conflict had been portrayed in many dreams that Alan had reported previously, in which he would be irresistibly drawn toward a roiling sea or into the eye of a storm. The conflict was revived and made more complicated during Alan's early adolescence when his mother became depressed again and would, for ill-defined reasons, join him in bed and he could feel the warmth of her body close to his.

Alan's mother's depression had been sufficiently severe that he had been sent away to live with an aunt for six months. His early experiences of being rejected and abandoned by his mother had been eclipsed in his memory by positive images of the care he had received from the aunt with whom he went to live. A kind of tacit collusion, almost a folie à deux, between Alan and his aunt was established, beginning during the time his mother had been disabled and lasting throughout his childhood. Alan's aunt totally idealized him and was unconditionally accepting of him, in return for which Alan did not contradict her fantasy that he was actually her son. Alan hoped to recreate with me the kind of mutual idealization he had enjoyed with his aunt. His experience of my hostile comment, disavowed but revealed through his slip, was that I was dashing his hopes. Instead of being sympathetic and accepting like his aunt, I was angry and rejecting, like his mother. Alan's childhood theory had been that his mother had become depressed and sent him away because his demanding jealousy and anger during her pregnancy had caused Gary to be stillborn. Now Alan thought I was punishing him for the demands and resentments toward me that I could see lurking beneath his superficial good-patient demeanor.

As these concerns emerged and could be reviewed, Alan's attitude toward women changed. He became less angry, and his preoccupation with sadistic fantasies faded away. He developed more comfort in his sexual life. For a time, he was tremendously excited by cunnilingus, and noticing this, realized that he was overcoming a longstanding horror and disgust toward female genitalia. One legacy of Alan's childhood misconceptions about the reasons for his mother's postpartum depression had been confusion about women's anatomy. The improvement in Alan's sex life brought with it an amelioration of his insomnia, and he discontinued sedative use altogether. We never did revisit and fully explore the reasons for my hostile tone when I made that pivotal remark to Alan, or his denial of the impact it had on him, but I do think we managed to successfully negotiate, tacitly, many of the issues that were brought up.

I treated Alan many years ago. Some things I would handle now quite differently than I did then. I'd like to think that I'd be more honest with myself about feeling and expressing hostility toward a patient and less likely to deny it, and that if I did act with hostility toward a patient and did deny it, I would not avoid discussing my hostility and denial when I subsequently became aware of them. But my reason for reporting Alan's treatment is not to illustrate optimal technique on my part.

The principle that I want to illustrate is that enactment is an aspect of all technique, good and bad. The comment that I made to Alan is a conspicuous example in point. My intervention expressed some not very admirable unconscious motivations. I was resentful toward Alan because he was frustrating me by not getting better, and I was competing with him in a self-pity contest. My critical remark, made in a tone that was less than kind, actualized Alan's most dreadful fantasy of once more being rejected by his angry, dissatisfied mother. Nonetheless, what I said to Alan proved very useful for purposes of his treatment. It created a crucial turn in the treatment that might never have occurred if I hadn't given expression to some of my very mixed personal feelings.

Interestingly, some time later I unexpectedly learned even more about the enactment dimension of my interaction with Alan at that moment in his treatment. In order to explain, it's necessary for me to mention a bit of personal background. When I was eight years old, my mother fell ill with a severe case of *myasthenia gravis*. Treatment for the illness was rudimentary then, and her condition deteriorated rapidly. Our family life shattered. I was devastated by my powerlessness to save either my mother or myself. On several occasions during my childhood, I had to stay with relatives because my mother was too sick to take care of me. A few years after Alan and I had concluded our work together, during my own personal analysis I became aware of some puzzling contradictions concerning my memories of the various times I had been unable to live at home. I actively questioned my father, who was still alive at the time, though my mother had died, about the details of when and where I had gone as a child. What I found out for the first time—my parents had never mentioned it— was that well before falling physically ill my mother had suffered a postpartum depression. It had been so severe that I had to be sent away for several months. This happened some time before I was two years old.

Imagine how I felt when I learned about the uncanny coincidence. I immediately thought back to Alan, and recognized that the self-pity and competitiveness that had motivated my pivotal comment to him had arisen from an unconscious traumatic memory of mine that had been *identical* to the unconscious traumatic memory that had motivated Alan's complaining. When I had asked myself who Alan thought he was, telling *me* about suffering, I had been completely unaware of the most important reason for my resentful self-righteousness: I knew exactly what Alan was talking about because I had gone through it, too! Enactment was an inextricable aspect, indeed, of what proved to be a very fortunate interaction between patient and analyst.

11

How to Get Out of an Impasse

Impasses in analytic treatment arise from all kinds of problems. Obviously, no single solution applies across the board. That said, however, there is a useful generalization to be made: the way out of an impasse almost always requires the analyst to be more explicitly candid than he or she has been previously.

I've discussed the advantages of an analyst's playing his or her cards face up (see Chapter 6). It isn't always easy to do, not least for the reason that there may be important cards that the analyst can't play face up because the analyst isn't aware of holding them. Unconscious elements of an analyst's personal psychology are always in operation and are very likely to be playing a key role when there is an impasse in treatment.

However, while an analyst can't know how unconscious parts of his or her personal psychology are implicated, an analyst can know that treatment is stuck. And though an analyst can't know what cards he or she is playing face down unawares, an analyst can turn all the cards he or she knows about face up. Doing so is usually a good option to consider when there's an impasse in treatment, even if turning all the cards face up that he or she can involves a significant sense of risk for the analyst. Here's what I mean.

ROBERT

Robert had been dissatisfied ever since he could remember. Outwardly, he seemed successful enough. He'd always done well academically. At the time he consulted me, he was in his second year at a prestigious medical school. However, Robert had always been uncomfortable with people. He had trouble making friends. Robert had the feeling he wasn't very likable, though he couldn't say exactly why. He had dated a bit. During his senior year in college, Robert met a girl who he thought would make a good partner in life; she was responsible and supportive. They decided to get married. When Robert talked about his fiancée, he didn't seem very excited.

Robert had been in treatment twice before. His first analyst had been extremely receptive, had always listened patiently, and had been consistently sympathetic and encouraging. After several years, Robert and the analyst had agreed that the treatment was a success and it was time to stop. Robert left with a fond feeling toward his analyst, but soon realized that the discomfort that had led him to seek treatment in the first place hadn't really changed. He then found a second analyst who seemed much more actively assertive than the first had been, which Robert thought would be a good thing. But Robert and his second analyst disagreed a lot. After a few months, the analyst abruptly discontinued the treatment. Robert never really understood the reasons for the analyst's decision. He only knew that the analyst had seemed angry and wouldn't discuss it.

As I got to know Robert, it wasn't hard for me to see why he was dissatisfied with his life and had trouble making friends. He was quite inhibited and rigid, but it was very difficult for him to admit it. Whenever I tried to call Robert's attention to problematic aspects of the way he operated in the world, he found ways to dismiss my efforts. There was a slipperiness about him; if I tried to get him to focus, he was rather easily moved to a kind of defensive contempt.

I could imagine why Robert's previous treatments hadn't worked out. It seemed probable that his first analyst had concluded that unconditional acceptance was all Robert could tolerate, which had made for a cordial relationship but no therapeutic benefit. The second time, Robert had apparently thoroughly thwarted and enraged his analyst, which was not surprising to me, given the rigidity, slipperiness, and contempt that I had encountered from Robert.

I tried to approach Robert's difficulties from every angle I could think of, but nothing worked. Robert was happy to come to his sessions. He could talk endlessly about his dissatisfactions, but I could find no way to help him look into the reasons for them. Robert seemed unable to try out new perspectives. After quite a while of sincere but unproductive effort, we were at a real impasse. Then the following happened.

One day, Robert began his session by describing an encounter he had just had with Marjorie, a girl in his class to whom he was attracted. "Nice dress," Robert said to Marjorie. "You should see what I'm wearing under it," she answered. Robert went on to talk about how much he had enjoyed the exchange and Marjorie's playfulness, and how proud he was about having been able to flirt with her. "But we both knew it wasn't going anywhere," he said. "How did you know that?" I asked, and Robert went on to explain to me, not for the first time, how he couldn't even imagine being unfaithful to his fiancée. He was committed and the wedding date had been set.

Now, in response to my question, Robert had explained why *he* ostensibly knew that the flirtation with Marjorie had no future; whereas in his original narration of the incident, Robert had emphasized how not only he but *Marjorie as well* knew it wasn't going anywhere. To my mind, this was no small distinction, inasmuch as I had gained the impression over time that Robert often obscured his crippling inhibitions and locked them into place by contriving to believe that a course of action that he had chosen to pursue had been the only available option. In other words, he frequently denied that he was making a choice, thereby depriving himself of the opportunity to examine the choice that he was, in fact, making.

This problem, which I had discussed many times with Robert, was particularly relevant to his romantic life. As we explored the feeling of dissatisfaction that had brought Robert back to treatment for the third time, it appeared to have to do in significant measure with Robert's anticipation of spending the rest of his life with a woman who really didn't interest or excite him. My own speculation was that Robert was irrationally frightened of being with a stimulating, potentially challenging partner; but we couldn't look into this or any other possible reason for his commitment to his fiancée, because Robert simply regarded the marriage as a fait accompli.

With all this in mind, I pointed out to Robert that he originally had said that not only he, but Marjorie, was sure that the flirtation wasn't going anywhere, and that it seemed that he had very little reason to assume Marjorie's unavailability, especially given what she had said to him. "In fact," I said to Robert, "I wonder if your own conviction that nothing could possibly happen between you and Marjorie depended, in part, upon your assumption—your very questionable assumption—that Marjorie wasn't up for it."

Then Robert did something that, as I saw it at least, he had done repeatedly in our work together: he engaged in what I considered to be revisionist history in such a way as to experience me as underestimating him, denying in the process his avoidance of looking at what he was doing, and shifting the focus from his own internal conflict to an interpersonal struggle that he tried to establish with me. "I didn't mean that she knew it wasn't going anywhere," he says. "It was my choice, I knew that." I asked him what significance, then, he gave to the way he originally described the situation, saying that they *both* knew. "Oh, I just spoke carelessly," Robert replied. I inquired whether Robert thought he was more comfortable with his choice to put on the brakes if he could ignore the possibility that Marjorie might be interested in him. "No, I don't think so," Robert said. "I can keep my eyes open about what I'm doing." I invited Robert to consider his intentions in commenting on Marjorie's dress in the first place. "Nothing beyond the obvious," was Robert's view. "I simply offered a harmless compliment."

I tried in a variety of ways to help Robert look into the incident further, but it all went nowhere. Robert now claimed that he had taken full responsibility all along for his way of participating in the interchange with Marjorie. He denied that he had ever claimed to have no choice about how to respond to her and about where he might try to go. Furthermore, he claimed to have had no conflict about the choice that he did make. Here was Robert's familiar slipperiness in full swing—and his defensive contempt as well, for Robert now added that I was trying to lay a trip on him; I was putting him down by seeing him as inhibited, and if he disagreed I would just insist that he was projecting his own self-criticism onto me.

"So there's nothing you can do," I eventually said to Robert. "I'm fucking you over and I've established ground rules that make it impossible for you to show me how I'm fucking you over." "Listen to your tone," Robert said. "You're angry." It was true; I was somewhat angry, and I thought about it for a moment. I responded, "Yes, I'm exasperated. In fact, you're really getting up my nose. It's very trying to be constantly cast—miscast, from my point of view—as a persecutor, when I think I'm trying to help you. Plus, as far as I can see, your negative view of me makes looking into the nature of your problems together impossible, which frustrates me."

Robert said, "But it's your job to contain your feelings, and look what you're doing!" I responded, "You know, Robert, if I were a less narcissistic individual, with less personally motivated therapeutic zeal, maybe I wouldn't get annoyed by you from time to time the way I do; maybe I'd be less irritated now. But frankly, I don't think it would make a terrific difference. On the whole, I think I'm pretty patient and good-willed toward you, and it seems to me that my narcissism and my susceptibility to becoming exasperated once in a while aren't really the major determinants of our problem here. I think the basic difficulty is that you are often unwilling to look at how you're making your choices. That's the way I see it, anyhow; and the real tragedy, in my opinion, is not that you unrealistically vilify me—which I think you do—it's that you're fighting like mad for the right to fuck up your own life by cutting off all your options without looking at how you're doing it."

"I think you're underestimating your narcissism, Owen," Robert said. "You're a bully. You can't stand it if I don't agree with you." "Well," I answered, "if that's really the case, Robert, you are truly screwed. It's always possible that I'm that oblivious to the extent of my shortcomings. But then, the question is, why do you stay in treatment with me? I'm not posing that question to talk you out of your criticisms of me, or to give you an ultimatum, or to encourage you to quit. I just want to point out how, once again, now in regard to our relationship, you've constructed your reality to be that you're miserable, and that there's nothing you can do about it. No choice."

"Yes, but that's my problem, Owen," Robert continued. "That's why I'm in analysis. You're supposed to tolerate your feelings about that, not get pissed off." I considered. "You mean, I'm supposed to accept you as you are? I'm not supposed to expect you to change, and not supposed to become frustrated if you don't change, and angry if the way you don't change involves constantly trying to blame me and vindicate yourself?" "Exactly," Robert replied. "Well," I said, "I don't think I'm capable of that, Robert. Frankly, I'm not sure I even *want* to be capable of that."

Robert stopped short. He was silent for a minute. "You know," he said, "there's something about you being willing to admit your own selfish interests and your own limitations that's weird to me. I've been thinking that you're a tyrant and an asshole, just like my father. But I know my father would never say what you just said. He'd never be honest about where he was coming from." Robert paused again for a moment. "Holy shit!" he said. "I just realized something. *I'm* being like my father. I'm doing just what he always did, saying, 'This is how I am. If you don't like it, fuck you. You've got a problem.' You know," Robert added, "I've always liked the fact that you don't automatically back down when I guilt-trip you. Actually, I think you usually can listen to criticism if you think it's justified; but if you don't think it's justified, you don't accept it. I even like seeing you get pissed off and knowing that you'll stick to your guns if you think I'm out of line. I wish I could have been that way with my father. Instead, I would doubt myself and think, 'Maybe he's right. I'm all fucked up.'"

This was the first time Robert had ever mentioned his father's take-it-or-leave-it stance and his own childhood reaction to it. For the rest of the hour, Robert explored how much he feared his hostility toward his father. When he was a boy, Robert had always felt that if he got angry at his father and stood up to him, it might provoke a fight that would either destroy Robert or disrupt the relationship with his father that he needed so badly. Eventually, Robert's thoughts returned to Marjorie. He considered his attraction to her and his worry that she wouldn't find him adequate—sexually or intellectually. That was why he didn't take the flirtation any further. Marjorie reminded Robert of the very beautiful, successful woman whom his father married after divorcing his mother. Robert was afraid that he couldn't be as big a man as his father, a man who could take on an exciting woman.

In the meetings that followed, Robert considered at length to what extent his sudden recognition of his identification with his father, his competition with his father, and his fears of being inadequate by comparison with his father, useful as they all were, had also served to avoid a showdown with me. He wondered how tolerant I was, really, of being challenged.

Two years later, Robert's treatment ended. He felt that he had benefited a great deal. It's always particularly satisfying when a positive therapeutic outcome takes unanticipated form, because it confirms that the patient has found the symptom relief he or she sought according to his or her own lights, and was not just complying with the analyst's expectations. Therefore, I was surprised and happy when our work did not result in Robert leaving his unexciting fiancée behind, as I thought it would. Instead, as Robert progressed, he discovered how much of what he had experienced as his fiancée's limitations had actually been the effect of his own inhibitions. Their life together became much richer in many ways. Eventually, they married, had children, and sounded quite happy at last report.

At the end of his treatment, Robert recalled the session I've reported and its importance to him. "I never would have believed that you really cared about me," he reflected, "if you hadn't been able to be honest about how I could 'get up your nose,' as you put it that time.

Also, I don't think I'd have felt okay about acknowledging my limitations if you hadn't been willing to take responsibility for yours."

In trying to find a way out of the impasse in which Robert and I were deeply entrenched, I applied what was essentially an extension of the principle I stated when discussing how best to fly blind (see Chapter 5): the only thing an analyst really has to offer, and the only thing a patient can really use, is the analyst's account of his or her experience of the treatment. In the case of flying blind with Robert, turning all the cards I knew about face up and giving him a full account of my experience was especially difficult because the experience that I had to be willing to describe to Robert was of a kind that is extremely difficult for an analyst to own, let alone to share with a patient.

I told Robert that I was fed up with certain things about him, I admitted to selfish interests on my part about which I did not feel apologetic, and I justified myself in the face of his criticisms. Furthermore, I used slang, obscenity, and in various other ways communicated to Robert the degree of my exasperation. These are unorthodox, highly questionable behaviors for an analyst; some people might even consider them unethical. It was with a very considerable sense of personal risk that I turned all my cards face up for Robert to see. It's easy enough to report it now, given the happy ending, but at the time I hadn't any idea where it would lead. I fully expected that letting Robert know my experience of our impasse might blow up the treatment. Furthermore, Robert was a member of the medical community and he was quite capable of trying to take action against me. At the same time, I knew that as things stood the treatment was going nowhere, despite the fact that I, like two analysts before me, had tried everything I could think of.

It is not all that uncommon for resolution of an impasse to hinge upon whether the analyst is willing to turn all his or her cards face up. Shame or fear on the analyst's part can be obstacles. So can the analyst's conception of proper technique. I thought it very likely that Robert's second analyst, whom I knew to be skilled and thoughtful, had gotten into the same kind of impasse with Robert that I had, and had reached a similar point of complete frustration; only that analyst's theory constrained him from the kind of radical self-disclosure in which I engaged. He tried to address the stalemate via interpretive comments that Robert was completely unable to use. Because he felt he could not turn all his cards face up, the analyst could only talk to Robert about who he thought Robert was, without telling Robert who he, the analyst, was. You can't get out of an impasse that way. It is characteristic of an impasse in analytic treatment that the patient's view of himself or herself and of the analyst does not accord with the analyst's view of himself or herself and of the patient. Unless and until analyst and patient can compare notes thoroughly concerning their views of self and other, they remain stuck; and it is the analyst's responsibility to be the first to push forward with candid self-disclosure, when necessary.

12

Patients Who Want to Destroy Their Treatments

The first thing to be said about patients who want to destroy their treatments is that such patients don't, in fact, exist. There are only patients who *seem* to want to destroy their treatments. In trying to understand what motivates a difficult patient, an analyst has to be careful not to fall into what is known in logic as the *teleological fallacy,* which consists of erroneously assuming that the *consequences* of an action reveal the *intention* that prompted the action. So, an analyst may feel defeated by a patient, but that doesn't mean that the patient was trying to defeat the analyst. Some patients wind up making treatment impossible with analyst after analyst, but that doesn't mean that the patients wanted their treatments to fail.

Freud unintentionally set the stage for misunderstanding when he developed the concept of a *negative therapeutic reaction* to describe cases in which a patient does not improve, or even gets worse, despite what appears to be productive analytic work. The concept of a negative therapeutic reaction is harmless enough when applied to patients whose problem is that they feel too undeserving to allow themselves to benefit from their treatments—that is to say, when unconscious guilt is the patient's root problem. On the whole, analysts, beginning with Freud, have been alert to the effects of unconscious guilt and can be helpful when unconscious guilt is indeed responsible for the trouble. However, when analysis does not confirm that unconscious guilt is the cause for a negative therapeutic reaction, analysts, following Freud's lead, start to think that the patient's failure to improve is motivated by *aggression*. They assume that treatment must be failing because the patient wants it to fail, and that the patient's actions express destructive or self-destructive motivations. Many psychoanalytic articles have been written about the role of aggression in negative therapeutic reactions.

The observation that a patient is bent on destroying his or her treatment is made from the analyst's point of view. Invariably, the patient has another intention entirely in mind, which the analyst has failed to understand. In these situations, the patient's motivations can be quite difficult to identify and are likely to have nothing at all to do with hostility or aggression.

ROGER

Roger was a talented young investment banker who suffered continuously in his treatment. He worked very hard to understand the reasons for his impotence and premature ejaculation, but the troubling symptoms persisted. Furthermore, Roger consistently experienced me as brutal and exploitive. Anything I said to him that was not an outright compliment or encouragement, he considered an assault. If I was silent, he was sure it was out of contempt for him. Roger frequently enlarged upon the sadism and greed that he perceived in my conduct toward him. To prove his points, he would quote me out of context, or assign malignant significance to my facial expression or to the subtlest nuance in my choice of words. Roger was much more interested in analyzing me than himself; but if I tried to point that out to him, he charged me with denying my irresponsibility and defending myself by taking the offensive. Whenever an episode occurred in which Roger thought my character failings were revealed with unusual vividness, he could be counted on to relate it in enthusiastic detail to all his friends.

At the same time, Roger was quite uninterested in discontinuing treatment or seeking another analyst. He claimed that to give up on me would be to admit defeat. He thought that I was enormously skilled, and he hoped to reap the benefits of my skill if he could get me to use it properly. I suggested to Roger that he seemed to be insisting that he could see the emperor's new suit of clothes; but this, too, he dismissed as a defensive evasion on my part. Roger clearly had an agenda that he was determined to pursue, despite the fact that it appeared to be yielding him nothing but pain, and his agenda seemed to have everything to do with the expectation of gaining something by defeating me. Naturally, when I invited Roger to consider this perspective on how he was approaching his treatment, he laughed at me.

Roger's attitude toward me was not entirely surprising, given certain parts of his history. His father and his older brother were both very high-powered lawyers. There had always been an atmosphere of intense intellectual rivalry among the three men of the family, all of whom considered themselves to be very special. They were treated as special, too, by Roger's mother, whom they, in return, looked upon with affectionate disdain as "a little flaky." Roger was his mother's favorite. He claimed not to have minded that position, rejecting completely the possibility that he might be worried that he was somehow too much like her. He insisted, as well, that the competition with his father and brother was just good sport—stimulating, rather than threatening or oppressive in any way.

Eventually, though, cracks began to appear in Roger's smooth idealization of life with his father and brother. He asked himself why they had always insisted on triumphing over him, even though he was the youngest. Roger reviewed his memories and began to realize that his father had only offered help when it made him look like a big shot; otherwise, he wasn't available when Roger needed him. Roger recalled, too, that his brother sometimes teased him with a terrible cruelty that went way beyond fun. We began to understand how Roger's childhood experiences had led him to feel weak and unmanly in ways that seemed connected to his sexual symptoms. He attacked me as a proxy, to revenge the many humiliations he had suffered. The attacks also expressed his determination to reform me as he wished he could have reformed his father and brother.

We explored other motivations for Roger's suffering, as well. Seeing himself as a victim of abuse helped relieve his guilt for having joined his brother and father in disdaining his adoring mother. It was also a punishment for having been her favorite. And deep down, Roger believed that if he submitted to me by faithfully attending his treatment, in the end he would be rewarded by being given a strength that I had and that he lacked.

Both Roger and I found these insights compelling. However, his sexual symptoms were not alleviated by the understanding we gained. Neither was his experience of treatment as an ordeal. Roger felt each new discovery about himself as a narcissistic injury perpetrated by me. He thought that what he was learning was true, but that it didn't help him, it only allowed me to feel superior. My own reaction to the way things were going was puzzlement, frustration, and concern that I was engaged with Roger in a costly and fruitless exercise.

That was the point we had reached when one day I dozed off during a meeting with Roger. It was the end of the day, I was coming down with a cold, and I was aware of feeling tired. But forty minutes into the session, I was paying attention and had my eyes open. The next thing I knew, I was awakening, somewhat disoriented, to the sight of Roger tiptoeing to the door. The clock showed that our time was up. I apologized confusedly and said that we would have to talk about what had happened.

Needless to say, at our next meeting I waited in considerable discomfort to hear what Roger would say. I anticipated that his castigation of me would reach new heights. I only hoped that I could keep my head, discuss my thoughts and feelings candidly with Roger, and try to turn what we were able to understand about the episode to some good account. However, when Roger began to speak, I was astonished.

He said that he knew he was an extremely trying, unrewarding patient. He imagined it must be infuriating and boring for me to have to listen to his repetitive complaints, and he thought that falling asleep was entirely understandable, under the circumstances. Moreover, as

Roger discussed his continuing reactions since the incident had occurred, I realized that he had not mentioned what had happened to any of his friends, which was truly exceptional! Obviously, Roger was eager to excuse me and to take responsibility for my lapse upon himself. He seemed to want to deny the possibility of even innocent frailty on my part: by now my voice was quite hoarse and I was blowing my nose frequently, but Roger made no connection between the appearance of these symptoms and my having fallen asleep.

Instead of vilifying me, Roger was protecting me. What was causing this complete reversal of his usual modus operandi? It began to dawn on me that it was the unavoidable reality of my misdeed that led Roger to treat it differently. I realized that his usual criticisms of me were caricatures *that were meant to be discredited.* No matter how vociferously Roger accused me of being hostile and out of control, he could rely on me to object because he knew that I knew he was distorting and falsifying. His friends were amused by his tales about me, but they understood that Roger was exaggerating and twisting the facts for effect. Now that Roger had actual evidence for his accusations, he disavowed them with all his might.

I told Roger what I thought about the dramatic change in his attitude toward me. I suggested to him that in the past when he criticized me he had again and again erected straw men that he knew would be knocked down. It seemed to me that his purpose in doing that must have been to convince himself that some negative view of me—which we did not yet know about—was only a product of his imagination and not really true. We had to find out what that negative view was and why he was so afraid of it.

The next time we met, Roger was obviously very upset. He stared fixedly at the floor, his face tense, and haltingly described that he had been terrified overnight by intrusive images—so terrified that at times he had thought of killing himself to make them stop. He kept picturing me with my arms outstretched, about to strangle him. It wasn't a hallucination, exactly, he knew it wasn't real; but he couldn't get it out of his mind. Somehow this image was linked with his longstanding fear of choking to death on a piece of food. Roger had mentioned that fear before in passing, but I now learned that there had been times when it had been quite serious. He had been afraid to eat and suffered from bouts of mild anorexia. Roger thought about how he avoided kissing women—especially active, strong women, to whom he was attracted—because of the way they forced their tongues down his throat.

Given the content of Roger's dramatically malignant image of me and his associations to it, I thought he might go on to expose a disturbing fellatio fantasy, perhaps related to the homosexual aspects of his rivalry with his father and brother; but again I was surprised. What poured forth was a torrent of new material related to his mother. From time to time, Roger had referred with amusement to his mother's attitude that no girl was good enough for her boys, but now he described his mother's wildly venomous remarks about any girl he or his brother even mentioned, and his mother's active efforts to sabotage her sons' teenage efforts to date. Also, his mother had so hounded his father with her pathological jealousy that she had to be forbidden to contact him at his office. The secretaries were given standing orders to hang up on her if she called. What Roger had termed "a little flaky" about his mother turned out to represent disordered thinking that could reach delusional proportions. She firmly believed that on several occasions she had left her body and traveled to other cities. Her fear of contagious illness was so extreme that she would only allow herself to be in a small enclosed space, like a car or an elevator, with family members. When Roger was ten years old, his mother had described to him in great detail a miscarriage she had before he was born, what the fetus looked like and how she flushed it down the toilet.

Over time, it became clear how much of his childhood Roger had spent being scared to death of his mother. He never knew when one of her pathological concerns would erupt or what would happen to him if he became the object of her fear and rage. She certainly saw men as special, but the frightening side of that was that she envied and resented men terribly. As her favorite, he could also be her prime target. He might get flushed down the toilet!

As a child, Roger couldn't live with his constant terror, and so to deal with his fears he adopted a strategy of convincing himself that they weren't realistic. He tried to believe that his terrifying image of his mother was an exaggeration and a distortion of who she actually was. In doing that, Roger was following the lead of his father, who denied the impact his wife was having on her sons and encouraged them to think of her as "just a little flaky." Roger's father, after all, made his living as a successful criminal lawyer by constructing ingeniously favorable interpretations of his clients' actions.

Roger devoted himself to the principle that *things aren't what they seem.* He looked for ways to prove that his mother was reliable and not dangerous. He had referred often during his treatment to his happy memory of how patient his mother had been with the encopretic problem he developed when he was in grade school. Now, thinking carefully about it, he had to admit that the problem had consisted of only one or two incidents and that he had managed to keep them secret. In college and business school, Roger was constantly missing deadlines, expecting that his teachers would penalize him. He borrowed money from friends, didn't pay it back on time, and worried that they would be furious. But the teachers didn't punish him and the friends didn't get angry. Without being consciously aware of what he was doing, Roger always calculated what he could get away with to a fine degree, making sure that the upshot confirmed that his fears of being hated and rejected had been misconceived. This had been the purpose, too, of Roger's suffering in treatment with me. It was another effort on his part to convince himself that his experience of being abused was imaginary.

As he was able to relinquish this very costly defense of denial through fantasy, Roger came to experience me as an ally rather than an enemy. He was able to face his anxieties more directly, especially his fears of women, and it was then that he could make real progress with regard to his sexual symptoms.

Roger was never trying to destroy his treatment; he was only trying to feel safe. His motivation was not fundamentally aggressive. On the contrary, it was libidinal: in his own way, Roger was preserving the wishful image of a loving and lovable mother. When Roger steadfastly rejected my efforts to help him and made outrageous criticisms of me, he brought his enigmatic problem into our relationship where it could be exposed and analyzed. Far from destroying his treatment, Roger's negative therapeutic reaction made effective treatment possible.

The same confusion between intentions and consequences that can lead a negative therapeutic reaction to be misinterpreted as an expression of destructive aggression can prevent other clinical phenomena, as well, from being properly understood. Certain disorders of love seem self-destructive when they are actually motivated by optimism. Some people select life partners who resemble their abusive caretakers from childhood so that they can replay their traumatic past experiences, hoping this time for a happier outcome. Even if what transpires is inevitably another disaster, that is not what was intended. Other individuals feel too guilty about sexual excitement for one reason or another to simply enjoy it. They have to arrange for an element of suffering as an appeasement whenever they achieve sexual pleasure, otherwise they feel in danger of being catastrophically punished. Their conscious experience is of only being attracted to people who treat them badly, as if the mistreatment itself were an exciting stimulus. But enduring mistreatment is actually a way of paying dues to insure safety. The fact is that these masochistic patients are inhibited. They are very attracted to people who do not mistreat them, but cannot allow themselves to be conscious of it. Sexual pleasure without suffering causes too much anxiety and they choose the least evil, as they understand it.

13

Post-Traumatic Stress

I used to have an office not far from a busy street in San Francisco. Occasionally a heavy truck would rumble by, creating vibrations you could feel and causing the windows to rattle a bit, but my patients and I were quite used to that and paid no attention. Then San Francisco experienced a very powerful earthquake, one that did more damage than any since 1906. Afterward, every time a truck went by I startled, thinking for a moment that it might be the beginning of another major shake, and I noticed that my patients did the same. For each of us, the magnitude of the startle response and its longevity was directly proportional to how traumatic the experience of the earthquake had been. My own experience had been relatively benign. I was swimming laps when the quake struck, and I only noticed a peculiar difficulty staying in lane for a while—I didn't even realize there had been an earthquake until I got out of the pool. Within a few days, my attention to the rumble of passing trucks returned to what it had been before. But one of my patients had been at the top of a skyscraper in an office that swayed fifteen feet in either direction for what seemed to him like an eternity; and another had been eating in a restaurant where a heavy chandelier had fallen, missing her table by only a few feet. It was months before either of them was back to ignoring the rumble of passing trucks.

Many post-traumatic symptoms are of this kind—hypervigilant responses to perceptions of possible danger in highly sensitized individuals. For example, while I was treating a twenty-two-year-old, his father died suddenly and unexpectedly from a heart attack. Then, two weeks later, my patient suffered restrictive pericarditis (from which he recovered completely) as a complication of the flu. Understandably, during the next year he worried about every little twinge he felt in the area of his chest. For this type of straightforward post-traumatic stress, the main ingredients of treatment are reassurance and sometimes medication to diminish the strength of the anxiety experience; analysis has little to offer. However, psychological factors frequently exacerbate and extend an individual's response to trauma; then, analytic work can make an important difference.

Disturbing dreams are often a prominent feature of post-traumatic stress disorders, and an individual's post-traumatic dreams can offer useful clues to the best clinical approach to his or her psychological struggles. In understanding post-traumatic dreams, there is every reason to retain Freud's conception of dreams as wish-fulfillment fantasies. We humans pursue pleasure and avoid displeasure according to a basic program of tropisms; and that program, hardwired into our central nervous systems, is the product of natural selection. It guides individual behavior in such a way as to promote species survival—we enjoy eating, and putting our hands in a fire causes us pain. Recent discoveries in neural science and evolutionary biology, which suggest that dreams are produced by off-line processing of survival-related information during REM sleep, are in no way inconsistent with the conception of dreams as wish-fulfillment fantasies. Our pursuit of pleasure and avoidance of pain in dreams, as in waking life, help us in problem solving and direct us in our adaptation for survival.

Therefore, we can look to the wishes expressed in dreams an individual has following a traumatic event to help us understand specifically in what way the individual has been traumatized and how he or she has attempted to adapt to the trauma. Some traumatic experiences and their effects are fairly obvious. For example, a person who has experienced loss will dream of the loss being repaired—people who have had limbs amputated dream of being whole; people whose loved ones die have dreams in which their loved ones appear, alive once more. But sometimes, an important feature of the traumatic experience is not obvious, and only by paying close attention to the wishes expressed in the patient's dreams can it be understood and addressed.

A young woman came home one day to find her husband in the entryway, dead from a heart attack. Following the tragic incident, she dreamt over and over of coming to her house, opening the door, and hearing her husband moaning in agony, somewhere out of sight. Frantically, she searched for him as his moans grew louder and more terrible. Eventually, she found him, just in time for him to die in her arms. One might think that this woman's post-traumatic dreams were, if anything, more awful than the traumatic event itself. But she had a particular reason for wishing that her husband's death had occurred as she dreamed it. When she was in the second grade, she came home from school to find her mother in tears and her father gone. She never saw him again. She'd had no warning of the breakup of her parents' marriage. She didn't understand why it had happened, and in her ignorance she imagined that she was somehow responsible. Later in her childhood, her beloved dog was accidentally poisoned. She awoke one morning and saw him lying lifeless in the yard—another sudden, catastrophic loss for which she was completely unprepared and for which she felt responsible in an ill-defined way. She wondered whether if she'd had some anticipation of her father's departure, or her dog's death, she might have been able to prepare herself for those catastrophes and to reassure herself that there was nothing she could have done to prevent them. The circumstances of her husband's heart attack had once again subjected her to the sudden loss of a loved one without any anticipation; but in her dreams, she had some time to get ready.

The most puzzling post-traumatic dreams are ones that appear to depict the traumatic event exactly as it occurred. The portrayal of events in the dream seems to include no alteration of the traumatic experience that would give a clue to how the dreamer wishes things had happened differently. These dreams raise a perplexing question: Why would anyone wish to accurately re-create a traumatic experience? The answer is that no one does wish to accurately re-create a traumatic experience, and that these dreams only *appear* to depict the traumatic event exactly as it occurred. Actually, there *is* an alteration of the traumatic experience, but the alteration is easy to miss because it is accomplished by *omission*. When someone has post-traumatic dreams that seem to accurately re-create the traumatic experience, it is invariably the case that the traumatic event, while it may have been terribly dangerous and frightening, is one from which the dreamer in fact escaped unharmed; and the way that the dream alters the traumatic experience is always that the portrayal of the traumatic event is incomplete: the escape from danger—the happy ending, so to speak—is omitted from the dream.

Seemingly accurate post-traumatic dreams are particularly helpful to an analyst because they point the way to a feeling of guilt on the dreamer's part that might not otherwise be obvious and that often plays a crucial role in perpetuating post-traumatic stress. When dreams that seem to faithfully re-create the dreamer's traumatic experience are part of a post-traumatic stress disorder, it means that the traumatic event has stirred up a preexisting fear of receiving punishment and the dreamer can hardly believe that he or she has escaped unharmed. In repetitively accurate post-traumatic dreams, the dreamer goes over and over the traumatic event in order to gain reassurance that he or she has really come out safely— in the same way that a soldier wears "the bullet that missed" around his neck. However, since the dreamer feels deserving of punishment, he or she is too guilty to enjoy a feeling of safety. Therefore, the escape from danger is omitted from the dream, and what is actually a reassurance turns into an ostensible torment. Knowing about the possibility of this kind of conflict between guilt and relief can help an analyst address the dreamer's post-traumatic stress disorder.

NINA

Nina was enjoying her evening out to dinner when her date, a doctor, was suddenly called away to an emergency. He asked Nina if she might find her own way home from the restaurant, and she agreed. While searching for a taxi, she was accosted and robbed. A very unsavory couple forced her into an alley and made her give over all of her money. They did her no physical harm, but to ensure their getaway they made her strip off her clothes, which they took with them. They also showed her a knife and told her they would find her and cut her pretty face up if she called the police. Nina stayed in the alley for quite a while, too terrified and humiliated to move. Eventually, she forced herself to go out to the street. Luckily, before long a police patrol car happened by. The officers wrapped Nina in a blanket, brought her to the station house, found her some clothes, took her report, and helped her call a friend to take her home. The perpetrators were never found.

Six months later when I saw her, Nina was still in the grip of a severe post-traumatic stress disorder, not controlled by medication. She was irritable, lethargic, and distracted. She was unable to work or to conduct a social life. She had lost twenty pounds and she was sleeping only three or four hours a night. She was afraid to close her eyes because she kept having terrible dreams in which she reexperienced the events of the robbery. She could smell the robbers' foul breath and feel how cold it was to stand in the alley naked. The dreams were accompanied by feelings of intense, mounting anxiety. Being rescued by the police was never part of them.

Nina was quite desperate, but she was not very self-reflective or very forthcoming. I had to piece together a picture of her by means of direct questions. Nina had always been popular and attractive, a prom queen in fact. I had the impression that she was an unconscious flirt who had to maintain to herself a pretense of total innocence. From her account of her family life growing up, it seemed to me that Nina had been her father's obvious and undisputed favorite, though she did not acknowledge that explicitly. Also, it was not hard to detect in

Nina's description of her relationship with her mother Nina's feeling that she had been the object of considerable jealousy and resentment. As a teenager, she had been annoyed by her mother's frequent, unnecessary warnings that Nina could get into trouble if she were not careful. Nina knew her mother was referring to boys.

After drawing Nina out as best I could for a while, I told her that we needed to understand why the events of six months ago were continuing to have such an impact on her, given that she had ultimately emerged from them safely. I said I thought she had been terrified because of the uncanny resemblance between the events of the robbery and the warnings her mother had always given her. Here she was, enjoying herself with a very attractive man, and look what happened. Maybe she dreamed about it again and again because she could hardly believe she had escaped. That rang true somehow for Nina.

We talked some more about how it had felt to be the apple of her father's eye, her awareness that he preferred Nina to her mother, and her discomfort with the situation. I pointed out to Nina how she only suffered in her dreams and never enjoyed the relief of being rescued. Nina replied that she might try to make her dreams less upsetting by seeing if she could get her memories of how the police had helped her to be part of them. I said I thought that was a good idea. It seemed to me that it must have been the guilt she felt toward her mother that prevented her from doing that in the first place.

This all transpired in the course of a few meetings. As a result of our conversations, Nina began to focus on a new aspect of the traumatic event: her date's irresponsibility in allowing her to go unprotected into the night. Even if he had to respond to an emergency, he could have given her a lift or taken a minute to make sure that she had a way home. Also, there was a change in Nina's view of her family. Her father, whom she had always seen as a kind of doting squire, began to come in for some criticism. Nina realized that his insensitivity and irresponsibility had played a role in creating problems between her and her mother. All in all, Nina seemed to become a little less complacently idealizing of men and their attentions to her and a little more sympathetic to women.

Symptom relief followed closely upon this shift in Nina's attitudes. Her post-traumatic dreams never did include her rescue by the police. Rather, what happened was that she began to have disturbing dreams much less frequently. She slept better, her mood improved dramatically, and before long she went back to work.

Even when dreams are not a prominent feature of a post-traumatic stress disorder, an unconscious conflict between guilt and relief can be operating in an important way. The same approach that I took in talking to Nina about her apparently accurate post-traumatic dreams can be applied to other post-traumatic symptoms as well.

OLIVER

Oliver had been given my name by a friend who was worried about him. When the police found Oliver wandering suspiciously on the Golden Gate Bridge, he admitted to being suicidal and asked them to call me. I met with him for the first time in the hospital emergency room to which he was brought. He was utterly desperate. Oliver's problem centered on disturbing flashbacks that plagued him continuously, to the point that he couldn't function at all.

Some months before, Oliver had gone to Asia on a business trip. He spent the last week of the trip in a beautiful Third-World city whose streets teemed with homeless, impoverished people. Oliver was intrigued by the place and took long, exploratory walks whenever he got the chance. He saw a great deal that was fascinating, and also much miserable suffering. At the time, he was aware of being moved and impressed, but not terribly disconcerted by his experiences.

However, once he returned to the States, Oliver found himself vividly reliving certain episodes from his travels that kept coming to his mind unbidden. He saw the faces of beggars who had importuned him insistently, felt them once again plucking at his clothes, heard their pleas in a language that he could not understand but whose meaning was unmistakable. In the recall Oliver experienced a dread that he had not felt originally. He was deeply distressed by the flashbacks. They distracted him and he slept badly. At first, he attributed his symptoms to travel fatigue, jet lag, or the culture shock of reentry to the West; but the flashbacks did not go away, and Oliver couldn't seem to pull himself together.

He saw several psychiatrists who diagnosed a post-traumatic stress disorder. They told Oliver that he was going over a bad experience in order to gain control of it. But that made no sense to him because he felt more out of control now than he had in Asia. A series of antidepressant, anxiolitic, and eventually antipsychotic medications were given extended trials at therapeutic doses. There was no improvement. By the time I met him, Oliver was at his wit's end.

In the history I took from Oliver, a couple of things came up that struck me as possibly significant in relation to his problem. One was that his business trip had been quite successful, as a result of which Oliver was now on the brink of becoming very rich indeed after having struggled for a long time to get his fledgling company off the ground. The other was that Oliver's younger brother, his only sibling, of whom Oliver seemed very fond, was something of a lost soul and had recently encountered disappointing reverses in his attempts to pursue a career in rock music. Oliver's star was rising as his brother's was falling, and Oliver got teary when he spoke about his brother's troubles.

In trying to relieve Oliver's post-traumatic stress, I looked to his flashbacks for direction. I thought of them essentially as waking post-traumatic dreams of the apparently accurate variety; therefore, I considered that they might function as reassurances, in a hidden and conflicted way. I began by pointing out the obvious to Oliver, namely that his flashbacks and the disorganization they caused were threatening to ruin the success he had achieved. When he agreed, I suggested that perhaps he didn't feel he deserved his success, especially given that his brother wasn't equally fortunate. The particular scenes that Oliver kept reliving might have seemed especially relevant in this regard—he may have felt guiltier toward the beggars than he realized at the time.

Oliver told me that what I said was not far from thoughts that had occurred to him. It was true that he was very uncomfortable about being better off than his brother, but he hadn't connected that with his flashbacks. Now that I mentioned it, though, he could see that the beggars did remind him of his brother in a way—he had the same bad feeling about not being more helpful. But Oliver thought he was entitled to the success he'd worked for so hard, and now these awful flashbacks were dragging him down. There seemed no escape.

I drew Oliver's attention to his choice of words and remarked that it was important that the experiences he re-created in his flashbacks were ones in which there had been an actual danger of being *dragged down*, literally, by the beggars, from which in fact Oliver *had escaped*. And I noted that the escape was never included in the flashbacks. It all added up, I told him, to the idea that he didn't feel he deserved to get away with being a success while others suffered. This idea struck him, and it led him to reflect on a certain temptation to flirt with disaster that he knew he felt. He had been advised not to wander throughout the city on his own, but he did it anyway.

Now it was possible for us to put together an understanding of Oliver's flashbacks as an effort to reassure himself that he had actually escaped the punishment he felt he deserved for superseding his brother, a punishment that he had sought out to an extent by putting himself at risk in Asia. In his flashbacks, he went over and over his escape from danger. But for the same reason that he did not feel entitled to his business success, Oliver did not feel entitled to enjoy a sense of safety; therefore, he satisfied his harsh conscience by deleting the happy endings of his memories, transforming them from reassurances into persecutions. The more Oliver tried to reassure himself, the more doomed he felt; and the more doomed he felt, the more he tried to reassure himself. Guilt won out over self-interest as the misguided loop went round and round.

Looking at his flashbacks in this way was very relieving to Oliver. It made sense to him; and it enabled him, for the first time, to see his flashbacks as something he was doing to himself for a reason, rather than experiencing them as a mysterious occurrence that simply had to be passively endured. He remembered that he had done well in Asia and that he had felt good—consciously, at least—at the time. Oliver began to regain a positive sense of purpose. He contacted his brother and discussed ways he could be helpful to him. Oliver's enthusiasm about his business returned. In subsequent visits, he reported that he was having flashbacks much less often, and when he did have them he didn't mind so much because he had a sense of what he was doing and why. I scheduled further meetings with Oliver, but we soon discontinued them, at his request. He felt on track again, business was great, and he knew he could get in touch if problems came up. As far as I know, they never did.

Nina and Oliver both suffered from obvious post-traumatic stress disorders. However, using the term *post-traumatic stress disorder* to describe their difficulties is only to say that in each instance a conspicuous precipitating event could be identified. Actually, all psychological problems can be understood to represent post-traumatic stress of some kind. Most often, the distress has not had a clear, abrupt onset, and no obvious precipitant can be identified. However, it was true for both Nina and Oliver that actual genesis of the post-traumatic stress disorder began long before a traumatic event occurred. In each case, an unusually disturbing experience caused a fracture along preexisting fault lines.

It is with respect to the predisposing factors, still in operation, that analytic treatment can be helpful—as it was in addressing the longstanding unconscious guilt that underlay Nina's and Oliver's post-traumatic stress disorders. Even when suffering is set in motion by unmistakable traumatic events of overwhelming proportions—for example, when post-traumatic stress disorders result from horrifying military combat experiences—individual psychological factors are important determinants. In the face of the same catastrophe, some people are more susceptible than others to becoming symptomatic. In the severest post-traumatic stress disorders, reassurance, medication, and analytic work are all part of effective treatment.

14

Phobias

Psychotherapists with different theories tend to make the same mistake that the blind men made when feeling various parts of the elephant: everyone believes that his or her theory is uniquely and wholly correct when, actually, competing theories are equally and only partially correct, each capturing an aspect of the truth particularly well. A good illustration is the way psychoanalysts conceptualize and treat phobias, as compared with the way behavioral therapists conceptualize and treat phobias.

Psychoanalysts theorize that a phobic patient's conscious fear is a substitute that the patient has put in place of his or her original fear, which remains unconscious because the patient doesn't want to think about it. The classic example is Freud's case of Little Hans, a boy who was afraid of horses. Investigation revealed that Hans was afraid that a horse would bite his penis, and further investigation revealed that Hans's fear of horses substituted for his original fear that his father would harm Hans's penis as a punishment for Hans's sexual interest in his mother. When the original, hidden fear was brought to light and discussed, Hans's phobia subsided.

Behaviorists, on the other hand, take phobias more at face value. Their theory is that if a patient has a snake phobia, it means that snakes elicit such intolerably strong anxiety in the patient that an avoidant response is mandated, no matter what the cost. The avoidant response can be extinguished in stages through the use of a systematic desensitization schedule, which begins by presenting the patient with a tolerable version of the feared stimulus and subsequently proceeds to more frightening versions in manageable increments. Initially the patient looks at pictures of snakes in a book, then the patient handles a dead snake, then observes a live snake in a glass cage, then pets a harmless snake, and so on.

What psychoanalysts sometimes overlook is that every clinical analysis can be understood as a desensitization process in which the patient learns to tolerate experiences that were previously intolerable—including thinking thoughts that were previously too threatening to be allowed into conscious awareness. A skilled analyst helps his or her patient fashion an incremental approach to threatening experiences that allows tolerance to build, just as a behavioral therapist does when arranging a desensitization schedule. That's how expansion of a patient's self-awareness is accomplished.

At the same time, behaviorists sometimes overlook the likelihood that what appears to be the patient's gradually increasing tolerance for the consciously feared stimulus is not the whole story. After all, some behavioral therapists are extremely successful while others are not, even when the same desensitization schedule is used. Why is that? Evidently, the therapist's manner in dealing with the patient plays a crucial role in determining outcome. Skilled behavioral therapists are somehow able, intentionally or unintentionally, to negotiate important corrective emotional experiences (see Chapter 5) with their patients; and those experiences may well have to do with the kind of unconscious fears that psychoanalysts have discovered, different from the conscious fears that are addressed by desensitization schedules.

Not only is it possible to apply a behaviorist perspective to psychoanalytic treatment and a psychoanalytic perspective to behaviorist treatment, but there is often overlap between the actual techniques employed in each. A clinical analyst will encourage a patient to "chal-

lenge" his or her phobia—that is, to push himself or herself to repeatedly confront the feared situation as much as possible. On the
other hand, a behavioral therapist will get to know his or her patient
and build a relationship while exposing the patient to a series of
stimuli. The best way to treat a phobia, it would seem, is to keep both
psychoanalytic and behaviorist theories and techniques in mind.

My work with Laura (see Chapter 5) began with alleviation of
her acute agoraphobia, but most of the treatment was concerned with
other symptoms. A clearer illustration of how a phobia operates and
how it can be addressed is the case of a toddler whom I treated for a
rather severe bamboo phobia.

TEDDY

When I was a psychiatric resident I was friends with a couple, both
of them university professors, who had an extremely precocious young
son named Teddy. During one of my visits, Teddy, who was eighteen
months old at the time, was playing with modeling clay, rolling it out
into long strands that he then chopped up into segments. I asked
Teddy what he was doing. "Hot dogs!" he exclaimed, pointing to his
creations. "Really? What else are they?" I asked tendentiously, being
an enthusiastic student of psychosexual development. "B.M.s!" he
replied. Just the kind of answer I was looking for, so I persevered.
"And what else are they?" "Penises," Teddy responded with a bright
smile, sensing that he had hit the bull's-eye, as far as I was concerned.
That was the extent of our exchange, for the moment.

Several weeks later, however, I got a call from Teddy's mother
who announced, somewhat humorously but also with obvious concern, "I've got the only kid in the world under two years old who's
asking to see his shrink!" Apparently, Teddy had for some time
seemed generally upset. He was irritable and uncooperative. Eventually, Teddy's distress became more focused. He began to speak
about "dangerous bamboo" and refused to go into the backyard,
which had previously been a place where he loved to play. There was
a small grove of bamboo in the backyard, but Teddy's parents were

completely puzzled as to why he should have suddenly become afraid of it. They were unable to reassure Teddy, and his fear seemed to escalate. He became reluctant to leave the house at all, evidently because he thought he might encounter "dangerous bamboo."

Teddy's parents were mystified and not a little frustrated by these developments. One morning, they insisted that Teddy accompany them to a picnic to which the entire family had been invited, but Teddy refused to get in the car. A terrific struggle ensued, in the midst of which Teddy exclaimed, "I want Owen!" Precocious as Teddy was, his mother knew Teddy didn't understand that I was a psychiatrist and that he needed psychiatric treatment; but whatever Teddy's reason for asking to see me, she hoped that perhaps I could be helpful, hence the phone call. My own first thought upon hearing what had happened was that the conversation I'd had with Teddy about hot dogs, B.M.s, and penises must have made an impression on him, connected in some way to whatever his problem was at the moment. So I agreed that I'd come over and see what I could do.

I knew Teddy's family quite well and I was aware that besides being both physically and intellectually precocious (Teddy ran around freely by his first birthday and was speaking complete sentences at fourteen months) he was precociously sexual. Teddy's mother had adored and envied her charismatic younger brother and she transferred certain of her feelings about her brother wholesale onto Teddy when he was born. If Teddy dropped food into his lap, she would say, "You've dropped something on your penis." She forbade anyone to play "Got your nose" type games with Teddy, lest he develop castration anxiety. One way or another, Teddy's mother helped him develop an excited, sometimes anxious focus on genitalia and genital activity. At eleven months, he was rubbing himself on the refrigerator, shouting "Hump!" to his mother's ostensible horror. Once when he urinated on the living room rug and his mother admonished him that he knew where he was supposed to do that, he replied, "Yah! In your vagina!" Some time later, he chanced to see his two-year-older sister sitting on the toilet. A horrified expression came over his face and he fled, shouting, "Gone!" It was established that he meant that his sister's penis was gone. He was reassured about the truth concerning genital differences, but for the next few weeks he kept undoing his pants and checking to see that he was intact.

I realized that it was in this generally overstimulating atmosphere that Teddy's bamboo phobia had taken shape. I knew, too, that Teddy's father had recently changed his work schedule and was now home a great deal more than he had been during Teddy's first year and a half. Inquiring into the events leading up to Teddy's difficulties, I found out that he had a while ago witnessed his father trimming the bamboo with a garden shears. I also learned that his father had tried to reassure Teddy that the bamboo was harmless by cutting a stalk to make a fishing pole for Teddy, which had only seemed to terrify him. And when Teddy's mother pointed out that a little sparrow was playing happily in the bamboo branches, Teddy had cried, "Oh, eagle!" with a stricken expression.

I began my efforts to be helpful to Teddy by sitting down with him on the floor of the living room and asking him how he was doing. He told me that a bad man was hurting people by banging nails into them, and also that a goose had bitten his finger. I tried to get Teddy to further explain these suggestive complaints, but he didn't elaborate. Instead, he took me by the hand into his room and closed the door. Evidently, he wanted more privacy.

Once in his room, Teddy began to play a game that he repeated endlessly during my first few visits with him. He had a coffee can filled with toy animals. He would pry the lid from the can, giving a short grunt, and strew its contents on the floor. Teddy set the animals up in various formations, saying all the while, "Fish live in the water," despite the fact that there were no fish in his collection. Then he would knock the animals over, and set them up again. As he did this over and over, his narrative expanded beyond, "Fish live in the water," to include, "Got knocked over," and eventually, "Fell off into the water."

By our third meeting, the picture had come together sufficiently for me that I could understand Teddy's play as a portrayal of his anxious fantasy about defecation. I told Teddy that I thought he was frightened that when he went potty his penis would fall off into the water like a B.M. or a fish and swim around there. Confirmation of my interpretation was dramatic. Teddy grinned delightedly and asked, "It won't?" Whereupon he promptly sat down on the potty in his room and produced a B.M., yanking happily on his penis all the while, repeating, "Won't fall off, won't fall off." Proudly, he showed me the B.M., then showed it to his mother, following which he stood by with interest while she flushed it down the toilet. As this was happening, Teddy's mother mentioned that recently his toilet training had been complicated by his refusal to flush his stools down the toilet or to be present when she did it.

The next time I came to see Teddy he indicated that we should meet in the backyard. This was, in itself, a bold alteration of Teddy's previous frightened retreat. He did carefully avoid coming near the bamboo grove that occupied one corner of the yard, and if I asked about the bamboo in any way he ignored me completely; but aside from that he marched around confidently, undertaking various projects of his own devising. Also, there was a decided change in Teddy's attitude toward me. Whereas before Teddy had treated me with deference, something like a respected critic he hoped would understand and appreciate the drama he was staging, he now seemed to take me for granted and to assume that I would obey and assist him in any way he liked as he went about his business. Most of the tasks Teddy set for himself had to do with damage and repair. He would dig a hole, then fill it up, giving me shovels to hold for him; or he would arrange a splint for a broken tree branch and order me to find string to tie it in place. Associated with my apparent descent in status was a marked increase in the degree of affectionate interest Teddy displayed toward his father.

My final visits with Teddy were taken up with his approach to the bamboo plant. As we played in the backyard, Teddy had often remarked, "Animals live in the forest," but I had not made much of it. Now Teddy's attention to the subject focused on the bamboo grove and the question of whether there was a bird hiding within it. Teddy told me that birds could bite, and could possibly bite his penis. He also made me understand that he had seen his mother's pubic hair and wondered whether there was something dangerous hidden in it. When, eventually, I asked Teddy whether he was worried that his mother and sister had lost their penises and would want to make him lose his, he once again enthusiastically confirmed that I had successfully verbalized his anxiety. "Yah!" he shouted. I reassured him at great length that women are very happy with their own, different genitalia and wished him no harm. It was then that Teddy led me to the bamboo grove so that we could inspect it thoroughly together and determine that it was certainly not dangerous.

After that, Teddy's phobic symptoms cleared up completely. I felt that I could stop meeting regularly with Teddy and return to the status of family friend and occasional visitor. We never spoke about hot dogs, B.M.s, or penises again, though occasionally Teddy would ask me to play catch with him in the backyard, and he always seemed especially gleeful when the ball rolled into the bamboo grove.

The genesis of Teddy's phobia and the way he and I were able to work toward a resolution of it fit quite well with a behaviorist conception. The bamboo plant itself became a frightening stimulus when Teddy saw his father cut it up with a garden shears. Teddy's preoccupation at the time with genital envy and damage violently colored his perception of the bamboo as an injured and vengeful being that he felt he had to avoid; and one aspect of Teddy's treatment consisted of a gradual approach to the feared grove in his backyard. At the same time, I was able to help Teddy approach some of the terrifying concerns that were informing his traumatic experience of the bamboo—his idea that he could lose his penis on the potty as he thought his sister and mother had, and later his worry that the women in the family were vengefully hostile toward his genitalia. Also, inasmuch as another aspect of Teddy's dilemma was his rivalry with a father who was newly returned to the family scene and interfering with Teddy's previously unquestioned preeminence, through his relationship with me as a father figure Teddy was gradually able to add elements of competition and aggression to his dependence. In each dimension, Teddy and I collaborated to arrange a step-by-step sequence of experiences that increased in tolerable increments his exposure to a feared stimulus. Similar processes of desensitization are at the heart of successful analytic treatment with patients of any age. Because of Teddy's eighteen-month-old simplicity, naiveté, and candor, the desensitizations were vividly explicit.

For the same reason, when looked at from a psychoanalytic perspective, the genesis of Teddy's phobia and the way in which it was successfully treated can be seen with unusual clarity. It was evident that Teddy's fundamental fears were of being harmed by his father or his mother and sister, but that it was easier for him to think about being harmed by a plant than to directly confront his conflicts about his loved ones. A crucial part of the incrementally increasing exposure that Teddy and I negotiated was his symbolic representation in play action of ideas that he could not tolerate thinking about directly, permitting me to articulate in verbal form for Teddy's conscious consideration thoughts that he was too anxious to allow into awareness himself. While this happens all the time in adult treatments, an analyst's interpretation of a warded-off idea, followed by confirmation from the patient of the correctness of the analyst's interpretation, is rarely as dramatic as it was when Teddy produced his B.M. or when he brought me over to examine the bamboo grove.

Teddy's phobia highlights the fact that in order for such a symptom to develop, a certain level of cognitive development has to have been achieved. Teddy's fear of bamboo communicated his anxieties in some ways and disguised his anxieties in other ways. The symptom could fulfill both expressive and defensive functions because Teddy was able to conceptualize how in some respects bamboo was the same as his father, mother, and sister (it could cut him; it could be damaged) while in other respects it was different (it was immobile outside his home; he didn't love or need it). In order to construct a phobia, Teddy had to be capable of simultaneously understanding similarities and differences. In other words, in order to be phobic Teddy had to be capable of *metaphor*.

I thought about this when I was trying to help Teddy resolve his problem because, according to what I was being taught about child development, metaphor should have been beyond the grasp of an eighteen-month-old. However, I was familiar with how far ahead of schedule Teddy was in so many ways, and I remembered an incident that had occurred some time before his fear of bamboo developed. We were all having dinner together and I asked Teddy if he wanted to go to a Chinese restaurant. "Yah! Eat puffa-puffa rice with pencils!" was his answer. For Teddy, chopsticks were and were not pencils. The lesson to draw from a precocious toddler's symptom and successful treatment is that phobias are always metaphoric, and therefore it's helpful if, at the same time as the patient is encouraged to gain more exposure in tolerable increments to the phobic object, the patient is also encouraged to consider that the phobic object both is and is not what she or he is afraid of.

15

Panic and Weird Feelings

One of Freud's enduringly valuable contributions was his recognition that *affects*, the basic repertoire upon which emotional life is built, are a set of signals that guide human adaptation. *Anxiety* denotes an important group of affects with which psychoanalytic treatment is intimately concerned. An anxiety is a signal of danger that occurs when an individual makes the judgment that a current situation that he or she is facing resembles an unpleasurable situation encountered in the past. Since it involves implicit recall of an unpleasurable situation, the experience of anxiety is, itself, unpleasurable; and because anxiety is unpleasurable, an individual's natural response to anxiety is to try to eliminate it. That is how anxiety functions as a guide toward adaptive action: the wish to eliminate anxiety motivates an individual to avoid danger.

For example, a woman grows up with an irritable mother who frequently loses her temper when her children make demands upon her. Later in life, when the woman thinks of asking her boss for a raise, the woman becomes anxious—she starts to tremble and feels a knot in her stomach, just as she did when she was a child and her mother yelled at her for being too demanding. She decides not to ask for a raise. If the woman has good reason to compare her boss to her mother, not asking for a raise saves her from getting fired. When the judgment of danger involved in an anxiety is valid, the effort to eliminate the anxiety is adaptive. However, if the woman's traumatic experiences with her mother have hypersensitized her (see Chapter 13) so that her anticipation that she would antagonize her boss by asking for a raise is unrealistic, she needlessly gives up making a reasonable request that would be in her best interests. Psychoanalytic treatment addresses maladaptive responses elicited by anxieties that are based upon invalid judgments of danger.

Sometimes a patient feels anxious, but has no idea what he or she is anxious *about*. The typical physiological signs of anxiety are present—racing pulse, perspiration, muscular tension, and so on— but the patient is not aware of any thoughts concerning a specific impending danger. The patient has a feeling of intense, even intolerable, ill-defined dread for no discernible reason. Such an episode is often termed a *panic attack*. Rarely, a patient suffers from panic attacks because of an underlying organic illness that produces the physiological phenomena associated with anxiety (e.g., *pheochromocytoma*, an epinephrine-secreting tumor of the adrenal gland), and it's important to consider this possibility when someone experiences episodes of terror with no apparent cause. Usually, however, a panic attack is a psychological symptom: it is caused by an anxiety in which the judgment of danger is one that the person who is panicking doesn't want to become conscious of, for one reason or another—perhaps it involves very shameful thoughts, for example.

When treating panic attacks, it's important to explain to the patient what is happening and to encourage the patient to overcome his or her avoidance of the thoughts that are producing the symptomatic state. Medication can help by turning down the signal strength, so to speak; but in order for the anxiety to be resolved, its ideational content has to be allowed into consciousness so that it can be evaluated. In this regard, panic attacks are similar to other symptoms that represent desperate attempts to avoid paying attention to threatening thoughts. Alan's intrusive nonsense phrases and obsessive-compulsive rituals (see Chapter 10) functioned in this way, and I approached them essentially the same way I would a panic attack.

Alterations in the sense of reality, termed *depersonalization* (the self is experienced as unreal) or *derealization* (the environment is experienced as unreal), are also symptoms that arise from an effort to keep the thought content of anxiety out of conscious awareness. Attention is focused upon a distracting perception—for example, the feeling that one is observing one's self from a distance, or that everything seems "off" in some way—so that attention cannot be paid to threatening thoughts.

PHYLLIS

Phyllis, a woman in her late twenties, suffered from disturbing episodes of depersonalization and derealization dating back many years. The symptoms were hard for her to describe clearly. She would get a vague feeling of being disconnected from herself and a disturbing sense that things were weird, not as they should be. When that happened at work, she couldn't function. If it was in a social situation, she had to leave abruptly and be by herself. Phyllis could never identify a precipitant for any of the episodes. She consulted psychiatrists who offered to treat her with medication, but she didn't want to take any drugs. Instead, to try to gain better control over her mind, she enrolled in a meditation program. At first she had trouble achieving the required mental concentration. After a time, it became possible, but the results were opposite from what Phyllis sought. When she was able to get into a meditative state, Phyllis started to feel increasingly estranged from herself. She even had the sensation of leaving her body and going far away. Once, she began to shake and had involuntary arm movements. It was as if she were outside herself, a helpless observer. What if she should pick up a hammer and hit someone? Phyllis became quite frightened and discontinued her meditation program. It was at that point that she came to see me.

Phyllis hadn't the slightest idea what might be causing her distressing symptoms. However, when I asked her about her life in general, it became clear that she was struggling with some significant problems. In particular, she was worried about the way she related to men. When Phyllis met someone interesting, she would quickly become infatuated and preoccupied with him. She could think of nothing else. Almost immediately, her investment in the relationship was huge; she would become impatient and be unable to restrain herself from throwing herself at the man, getting ahead of herself in her assumptions. Knowing that she was driving the man away and hating herself for it, she was nonetheless unable to control her behavior.

Phyllis believed that she was messed up as far as men were concerned because of what had happened in her family when she was growing up. She was deeply bitter toward her mother for the way her mother adored Phyllis's older brother and constantly criticized Phyllis. Phyllis tried to deal with the situation by becoming pals with her father, but, unfortunately, when she was ten years old, her father became severely depressed and never really recovered. Phyllis's brother, whom she both resented and admired, always acted coldly superior toward her, spurning her efforts to be close to him.

Over our next few meetings, Phyllis explored her troubles with men in more depth than it seemed she had originally intended. In the course of discussing the way she always wound up feeling hurt by her boyfriends, Phyllis began to have "that weird feeling." She could make no connection to any threatening ideas stirred up by what she had been talking about. Things just seemed unreal, almost as if everything were two-dimensional and in black and white. I encouraged Phyllis to pursue her associations to the visual changes she was experiencing. She had a train of thoughts connected to black and white. First, she found herself thinking of a poster she had seen, advertising an interracial organization—black and white hands clasped. This led her to describe a series of affairs she'd had with African men in which she felt she had let herself be abused. She was ashamed about that. Then what came to mind was the color red in the middle of all the black and white. She was having her period, she said. She thought of when she had first menstruated, and how, at the time, she could have had a better relationship with her brother if she had let him abuse her. She remembered how he would tell her frightening stories at bedtime. He would put his hand over a flashlight and project a huge shadow on the ceiling. She remembered staring at it, being scared but also excited. The two-dimensional, black and white appearance of things was like that shadow.

Phyllis left her remark about the possibility of an abusive relationship with her brother unexplained. I told her that it seemed obvious that she had touched upon something important connected to her childhood relationship with her brother, and that she was now trying not to think about it. Her derealization experience was an avoidance maneuver, and her associations had led her back to the thoughts she had been trying to keep out of consciousness. Fixing her attention on the perception of things being flat and in black and white distracted her from thoughts she didn't want to think now, in the same way that staring at the shadow her brother projected on the ceiling had distracted her attention from things she didn't want to think about when she was young.

Phyllis got very upset. Between choking sobs, she told me that she was terribly ashamed of something that she had never told anybody about. There had been a period of several years, around the time of her puberty, that she had engaged in sex play with her brother. She had let him seduce her because it was the only way she could get him to want to be with her. He had tried to have intercourse with her, though she was never sure at the time whether he had actually been able to enter her. The whole thing had been frightening and confusing to Phyllis as a child, and still was when she recalled it now. Once, while her brother was getting her to fondle him in their backyard, they were observed by a passerby, who shouted at them. They were terrified and never engaged in sex play again. Her brother refused to talk about what had happened and returned to his former aloofness.

In our subsequent work together, Phyllis realized more about her hostility toward men and her covert sense of triumph over them. In sex, when the man had an orgasm, Phyllis would feel as if she had drained him of his strength and taken something from him. Reviewing these vengeful wishes and the anxieties they caused her permitted Phyllis to gain more balance and comfort in her relations with men. Her romantic life improved considerably, and she was no longer troubled by episodes of depersonalization and derealization. During one of our last meetings, as Phyllis was thinking about not seeing me any more, she began again to have the weird feeling. "I'm trying to distract myself from something," she said, and proceeded with some embarrassment to tell me how much she thought she would miss me and how she wondered whether I would miss her. Besides telling Phyllis that, indeed, I would miss her, I said that I was very happy to see that she had overcome her traumatic experiences with her brother to the point that she could let me know that she felt close to me without being terrified that I would either abuse her or reject her.

Phyllis's episodes of depersonalization and derealization were her ways of trying to remain unaware of shameful, frightening thoughts about being a victim and a perpetrator of abuse. She avoided being conscious of those thoughts by keeping her attention fixed upon certain perceptions that she brought to mind—a technique that she had used ever since childhood, when she stared at the image projected on the ceiling and tried not to pay attention to what her brother was doing to her. When eventually Phyllis became able to tolerate thinking about what frightened her and made her ashamed—her childhood sexual play with her brother and the powerful mixed feelings it stimulated in her—she no longer needed to depersonalize and derealize. The symptoms of depersonalization and derealization had been what Freud termed *defenses* against anxiety.

A *defense* is a psychological response elicited by an unpleasurable affect, aimed at avoiding experiencing the affect. Defenses that involve denial, distraction of attention, or other wholesale measures taken to prevent awareness of an unpleasurable affect altogether, are nonspecific; they can be elicited by any unpleasurable affect of sufficient intensity. Often, a patient who is symptomatic because he or she is employing such a defense will appear to be seriously disordered. On the basis of her strange perceptions and out-of-body experiences, the psychiatrists whom Phyllis consulted viewed her as incipiently psychotic and wanted to treat her with powerful medications. Alan's outbursts and compulsions led him to be misdiagnosed with Tourette's syndrome (see Chapter 10).

16

Worries versus Regrets

The defenses against unpleasurable affect involved in dramatically disruptive symptoms like Phyllis's (see Chapter 15) or Alan's (see Chapter 10) are usually last-ditch general emergency measures, so to speak. But there are other defenses that become involved in symptom formation that are less conspicuous, and that are *specific to particular unpleasurable affects*. In analytic treatment, it's crucial to try to be as clear as possible about which particular defensive maneuvers are in play and about which particular unpleasurable affects are being defended against, because the purpose of practical analysis is to help the patient eliminate the maladaptive affect-defense responses that produce his or her symptoms.

Inhibition is a defense elicited by anxiety. Inhibition consists of giving up or altering the effort to fulfill a desire when it seems dangerous to continue to pursue the desire. An anxiety warns of a danger; therefore, changing course so as to avoid the danger puts an end to the experience of anxiety. The woman who decided not to ask her boss for a raise (see Chapter 15) was inhibiting herself in order not to feel anxious. A phobia is the classic example of an inhibitory symptom driven by anxiety. Teddy's bamboo phobia (see Chapter 14) was produced by inhibitions. When Teddy's father suddenly appeared as a frighteningly powerful male presence in the world in which Teddy had previously reigned supreme, Teddy concluded that he had better give up acting like a masculine big shot. He stopped being sexually assertive toward his mother and sister, no longer claimed the backyard as his own special domain, and started worrying about getting hurt.

The typical sequence in analytic treatment is first to identify a defense, then to investigate the affect that elicits the defense. In the case of anxiety-driven symptoms, that means first recognizing an inhibition, then exposing the unrealistic anxiety that motivates the inhibition: the analyst notes what seems to be an unwarranted renunciation of pleasure on the patient's part, then helps the patient expose and review the judgment of danger responsible for the renunciation. The patient revises his or her unrealistic judgment of danger by correcting a misunderstanding formed in the past. For example, Diane realized that her belief that she was unfit for positions of responsibility was based on her misguided idea that she had been irresponsible toward her diabetic sister (see Chapter 9), and Margaret and I discovered that she was afraid that if she conducted an enjoyable social life she would lose her sense of connection to her depressed mother (see Chapter 8).

Besides anxiety, the other major category of unpleasurable affect commonly dealt with in psychoanalytic treatment is *depressive affect*. Whereas anxiety is a signal of danger, that is, of the *possibility* that a calamity could take place in the *future*, depressive affect signals the *certainty* that a calamity has occurred in the *past*. The prototypical event that causes depressive affect—the instance originally studied by Freud in his famous essay "Mourning and Melancholia"— is the loss of a loved one. Inhibition cannot be used as a defense against depressive affect, since altering course does not enable one to avoid an unpleasurable event that has already taken place. Instead, the defense elicited by depressive affect consists of an effort to *repair* the damage that has been done. Anxiety produces *worry* and an effort to *avoid* harm; depressive affect produces *regret* and an effort to deal with harm *already* done.

The symptoms of *depression* are not expressions of depressive affect; they are defenses against depressive affect, responses elicited by depressive affect. Just as is the case with anxiety, the capacity of depressive affect to elicit defense can be adaptive. The very same defenses against depressive affect that can produce the symptoms of clinical depression can be useful, when they occur within certain limits. Depression is often characterized as a "cry for help." Normal mourning also involves a constructive cry for help—a period of social withdrawal, apathy, self-involved preoccupation, even hopeless sadness that allows the mourner time to explore and come to terms with his or her loss, while communicating to others a need to be supported by them. The response to depressive affect represented by normal mourning is adaptive. When that response is too severe or continues too long it becomes maladaptive; then it is termed *pathological mourning*. Or, if it is an unrealistic sense of loss that produces depressive affect and elicits reparative defenses, what we see is symptomatology in the form of *clinical depression*.

Psychoanalytic treatment is often concerned with maladaptive defenses against depressive affect. When the symptoms produced are severe, it is difficult for a patient to participate in an analytic investigation. Medication can help by diminishing the intensity of a patient's depressive affect, allowing the patient to feel less desperate and more able to look at his or her maladaptive responses. Often, these consist of unrealistic efforts at repair. For example, Freud's study of *melancholia* (clinical depression in which self-reproach is a prominent feature) showed how an individual can seek to repair a calamity by living out a magical fantasy: the melancholic individual maintains the belief that a lost loved one is still present as part of himself or herself. This sort of irrational fantasy is a very costly defense against depressive affect.

I once treated a young woman whose life was being ruined by her constant hypochondrical worries. She spent all her time visiting doctors, sure that there was something wrong with her. I had the impression that she imagined herself to be ill in order to feel close to her mother, who had died several years before, after suffering from a terrible chronic affliction. For quite a while, the young woman ridiculed my suggestion that her hypochondriasis was part of her attempt to maintain an unrealistic fantasy of being somehow with her mother, until one day she realized that she was continuing to carry her mother's credit card around in her wallet, despite the fact that it had long since expired!

Just as an unrealistic judgment of danger produces maladaptive anxiety, an unrealistic judgment of loss produces maladaptive depressive affect. For example, sometimes a patient's depressive affect arises from a judgment of hopeless defeat that is itself the product of repeated failures due to inhibition. When that is the case, it is necessary to deal with the patient's depressive affect and the defenses it elicits before the patient's inhibitions and the anxieties that motivate them can be analyzed. Ellen was depressed (see Chapter 3) because she believed that she was doomed romantically. Her belief was based on her experience of relationships with men never working out. It turned out that her unhappy history with men was due to deep-seated inhibitions, but those didn't come to light until well into her treatment. It can also happen that a patient's inhibitions make the patient appear depressed, when the patient is actually struggling with anxiety. That was true, to an extent, of Ralph (see Chapter 2) and of Robert (see Chapter 12), both of whom were unhappy because they were fearfully relinquishing important pleasures.

It can be difficult to know at any given moment whether the leading edge of a patient's problem has to do with anxiety or depressive affect. In practice, the determination is made through trial and error. An analyst tries to address what seem to be the patient's inhibitions, and when that doesn't work, the analyst tries to address what seem to be the patient's magical reparative fantasies, or vice versa. Judgments concerning progress or lack of progress toward symptom relief guide the analyst's decision about whether to pursue one path or the other (see Chapter 3).

TODD

Todd was a brilliant young architect who sought treatment because of a problem he was having on the job. After graduating at the top of his class, he had obtained a sought-after position with an extremely prestigious firm. There, he did excellent work and was given rapidly increasing responsibilities. Eventually, he was put in charge of an important project. Now, it was his role to develop an overall conception of the task, rather than to pursue a direction someone else had established. Suddenly, for the first time, Todd was unable to concentrate and felt devoid of ideas. His career was seriously threatened by this puzzling impairment.

When he was growing up, Todd's mother had rather conspicuously favored him over his older brother. Todd was an outstanding student and his mother, who was very much an intellectual, took great pride in Todd's achievements and loved to discuss their shared interests with him. Todd's brother, more an athlete than a scholar, was excluded. Todd always felt guilty about this and kept as low a profile as possible when he and his brother were together. Todd deferred to his brother whenever he could.

It seemed likely that Todd was motivated to sabotage himself at his firm by a guilty fear that if he achieved too much in his own right it would harm his brother. As long as Todd could feel that he was a subordinate, his anxiety was held in check. It made him comfortable to defer to a teacher or a boss, as he had to his brother. But that element of defense was removed once Todd was promoted to a leadership position, and he had to take more drastic measures in order to avoid being too successful.

This view of Todd's symptom as an inhibition driven by anxiety appeared to be confirmed by the first dream that he reported in treatment. In the dream, he was in a foreign city. He saw a woman sitting alone at an outdoor cafe. She was terrific—sexy, intelligent-looking, sophisticated. He was attracted to her and started walking toward her. He became confused. He didn't know the language. What would he say? Which direction did traffic come from in this country? He could get hurt crossing the street. A handsome older man was there who knew his way around. Todd asked him for help. The man was friendly and seemed to want to be of assistance, but there was something amiss. Was the man attracted to the woman too? Perhaps the man was a homosexual. At that point, Todd awoke.

In the dream, as in waking life, Todd gave up what he wanted because he was afraid. He deferred to a rival. In his associations to the dream, Todd thought about the traffic coming from an unusual direction, as it does in the United Kingdom, and mentioned that the city looked like London. In fact, then, Todd could speak the language, which made it even more obvious that he was abdicating his capacities. I pointed out to Todd the possible parallel between his dream and his symptom: he felt the need to claim that he could not do things that he was actually quite capable of doing, in order to permit someone else to supersede him. I wondered with Todd whether he was guiltily afraid of being punished if he were successful in a way that his brother was not. Perhaps his sudden incapacity at work was an extention of his longstanding need to keep a low profile.

Todd eagerly accepted and pursued the line of thought that I proposed. He thought a great deal about his feelings toward his brother, and produced thoughts and memories that confirmed my hypothesis that he was inhibiting himself on the basis of guilt. Nonetheless, his symptom at work persisted. He found a way to diminish the need to take a leadership role by involving a senior partner in the project. For the moment, significant damage to Todd's career was averted, but the solution was not one that could continue to be employed.

As we continued to try to understand what was happening, I was struck by a couple of aspects of Todd's participation in his treatment. For one thing, he was extraordinarily patient. Despite the lack of progress toward symptom relief, Todd didn't complain or worry and expressed an attitude of confidence in me and in what we were doing. Also, I realized that Todd deferred to me in our work together, in the same way that he deferred to his senior colleagues on the job. If I suggested an idea—for example, that he might be limiting his professional success out of guilt toward this brother—Todd took it up with enthusiasm, but he never broke new ground at his own initiative. Todd was very bright and thoughtful, and his manner of letting me take the lead was rather subtle; so it was a while before I caught on.

I shared my observations with Todd and suggested to him that he seemed to feel that he had to follow me, rather than to direct himself to where he needed to go. What I said made him quite uncomfortable. Eventually, Todd had another dream that revealed more about the nature of his discomfort. In the dream, he was pregnant. He was still a man, but he had a baby growing inside him. He wanted very much to give birth and he couldn't figure out how to do it. Where would the baby come out? Evidently, Todd's deference to me, and his patient confidence despite the lack of symptom relief, proceeded from a fantasy of magical repair that was shaping his experience of our relationship and the treatment. He was waiting for me to impregnate him, so to speak, so that he could develop the capacities he lacked and needed in order to be a leader.

The fantasy was a defense against depressive affect, caused by Todd's idea that he was missing certain essential masculine characteristics. Todd brought forward his longstanding certainty that being too involved with his mother growing up had made him less of a man than his brother. He recalled scary, embarrassing homosexual thoughts from his childhood of wanting to get closer to his brother in order to be strong like him. Once Todd's fantasy of magical repair and the depressive affect that instigated it were addressed, Todd could go on to explore the inhibitions and anxieties that underlay his ideas about being unmanly. His mother's conspicuous favoritism had led him to feel guilty toward his father, as well as toward his brother. Todd believed he didn't deserve to be victorious. On that basis, he had always feared that he would only make a fool of himself if he tried to be too much of a man. To a certain extent, of course, this anxiety and resulting inhibition had become a self-fulfilling prophecy. That was what was happening now, again, at work.

Our efforts to investigate Todd's problem at work led us to think first about inhibition and anxiety, then about magical fantasy and depressive affect, then again about inhibition and anxiety. This sort of back and forth, guided by progress or lack of progress toward symptom relief and other accumulating observations, is not at all unusual and can occur any number of times as a treatment proceeds.

All things taken together, it's generally easier for an analyst to deal with a patient's inhibitions and anxieties than a patient's fantasies of magical repair and depressive affect. When a patient is inhibited, he or she relinquishes pleasure in the face of perceived danger. The analyst's task, then, is essentially to encourage the patient to pursue pleasure and to be less afraid—the analyst functions as a mentor or rooting section, so to speak, which is something most of us like to do. That was the case, for example, when I helped Margaret become more socially active (see Chapter 7). On the other hand, a patient who is entertaining a fantasy of magical repair is pursuing pleasure, though the pleasure is based on illusion and doomed to end in disappointment. Then, the analyst's task is to deprive the patient, at least for the moment, of the anticipation of pleasure—to help the patient realize that he or she is waiting for Godot, or that no one will pay up on the IOU's the patient is trying to cash in—and none of us likes to do that. My argument with Robert (see Chapter 7), for example, was largely concerned with my attempt to confront him with his unrealistic expectations and the passivity they engendered.

Often, contending with a patient's fantasy of magical repair is quite trying for the analyst. When a patient is struggling with depressive affect and defenses against it, in order for the treatment to get off the ground the analyst may have to collude, perhaps unconsciously, with the fantasy of magical repair as it influences the patient's experience of his or her relationship with the analyst. Later, when it becomes necessary for the analyst to expose as unrealistic the patient's magical fantasy about the treatment relationship, the patient believes, with some justice, that he or she has been seduced and abandoned; and the analyst, also with some justice, agrees and feels guilty. That certainly happened in my treatment of Alan (see Chapter 10).

17

Oedipus Revisited

It is not unusual to hear a psychoanalyst's theory criticized on the grounds that it's merely an expression of his or her personality. It should be obvious that such criticism is a species of ad hominem argument and has no merit. Of course, *all* psychoanalytic theories, valid ones as well as invalid ones, express the personalities of the analysts who propose them; therefore, it's nonsense to discredit a particular psychoanalytic theory on the basis of its having subjective origins. It's probably useful, too, to keep in mind that all psychoanalytic theories have subjective origins; it helps to prevent any of them from being idealized.

What interests me is that skepticism about a psychoanalytic theory based on the idea that it's too much an expression of the theorist's personality usually arises when a *new* theory is offered. One hardly ever hears *Freud's* ideas questioned because they were expressions of his personality. Take, for an example par excellence, Freud's ideas about sexuality. They're practically sacrosanct to psychoanalysts. And yet, there's much to suggest that Freud was significantly uptight about sex. When he was thirty-nine years old, Freud wrote in a letter to a friend that he was much relieved to have left the troublesome matter of sexual life behind. Neither Freud's experience of relief at the waning of his sexuality, nor the relatively early age at which it waned, are what most people, I think, would consider signs of erotic mental health. Furthermore, Freud was subject to fainting fits and a variety of other hysterical symptoms of a kind that he himself understood to result from excessive sexual repression. Freud was notoriously indifferent to music, even phobic about it: he refused to allow a piano in his London apartment. And he pathologized what he termed "oceanic feelings." It seems Freud may have been uncomfortable with the Dionysian side of life, the measure of relinquishment of control and loosening of individual boundaries that is involved in ecstatic pleasure.

Clearly, these are only conjectures. But we *can* be sure that Freud's theories about sex expressed the personality of the theorist—as all theories do—and we have every reason not to *rule out* the possibility of considerable neurotic difficulty with sex on Freud's part. In any case, we can't be surprised that Freud's theories about sex were brilliant in some ways and flawed in others. Freud had a genius for appreciating the plasticity of sex, its transformations and protean manifestations, and for recognizing the importance of infantile sexuality. What is most questionable about Freud's thinking about sex is the nearly totalitarian position he gave it in his theory. For instance, the deep intellectual rift between Freud and Jung was fundamentally concerned with the role of sexual instincts in human motivation. Freudians usually attribute the disagreement to Jung's mystical bent and what they see as a related need on Jung's part to deny the all-importance of sexuality. But the argument can at least as easily be made that Jung, whose personal sexuality may have in fact been healthier than Freud's (it certainly did not undergo the same premature demise that Freud's did), was less susceptible than Freud to feverish overestimation of sexual motivations. Perhaps Jung had a reasonable perspective on the very important place of sexuality in everyday life, while Freud exaggerated it.

In this context, it's worth reviewing a particular component of Freud's theory of sexuality: namely, his proposal that the Oedipus complex describes a universal phase of normal psychosexual development. It was Freud's belief that every boy wants to sexually possess his mother, totally and exclusively, and necessarily sees his father as a rival to be eliminated. But a boy also loves his father. Therefore, according to Freud, the boy faces a dilemma that is tragic (which is why Freud named the complex after a Greek tragedy) because a completely happy outcome is not possible: either the boy must defeat and humiliate a father whom he loves, or the boy must submit to humiliating defeat himself. Of course, Freud postulated a corresponding dilemma for girls; but for the moment I'll speak about boys—for simplicity's sake and because that's where Freud began.

It's important to recognize that underlying Freud's conception of the Oedipus complex is his assumption that love within the nuclear family is a zero–sum game. It's as if there's not enough of mom's erotic attention to go around. Sharing mom erotically, with both father and son being satisfied, each feeling special in his own way, is not an option, in Freud's view; there has to be a fight to the finish between father and son—one winner and one loser. The optimal outcome, Freud thought, is that the boy loses the fight but consoles himself through identification with the aggressor: that is, the boy develops an ambition to be like his father; one day he will possess a woman and defeat all rivals (including, of course, his own sons, if he has any).

Now, this experience by a boy of his family situation as desperately competitive is certainly what we see, for example, when narcissistic parents pursue their pleasure without consideration for their son's needs; or when a father feels neglected following the birth of a son and becomes jealous of his wife's attentions to the son; or when a mother is disappointed in her husband and confides her disappointment to her son, conveying a wish to be rescued; or when various other problems in the parental love relationship occur with consequences for the child. Certainly, such problems are common. They may well have existed in Freud's family. But they are by no means *universal*.

In my clinical work, I've found that boys whose parents have a happy, passionate relationship and are loving toward their son do not seem to struggle with an Oedipus complex. When domestic conflicts don't create a competitive atmosphere, a boy enjoys a gratifying, appropriate sexual element to his relationship with his mother, is satisfied with it, and doesn't experience his father as being disturbed by it. The boy identifies with his father—not because of a need to identify with the aggressor, but out of a nonconflictual admiration for his father and desire to emulate him. For girls, successful psychosexual development without significant oedipal conflict is perhaps even more common because—in most western European cultures, at least— greater latitude for homosexual expression is given to females than to males, so that a girl, even more easily than a boy, can enjoy a measure of normal and appropriate sexual pleasure with both parents. My impression is that the Oedipus complex is by no means an inevitable component of normal psychosexual development, but rather is a consequence of certain not uncommon family problems that can have an impact upon a child's experience.

Despite the questions that can be raised about it, the concept of an Oedipus complex has become a cornerstone of psychoanalytic theory. Adherence to tradition makes analysts reluctant to critically review Freud's conception, even when they are uncomfortable with it. Some analysts have tried to mitigate the disadvantages of the concept by expanding it. They emphasize that the Oedipus complex has to do with relationships, and try to move the focus away from sexual rivalry, toward thinking of the oedipal stage of development as the time when a child moves beyond the parental orbit into true socialization. This perspective describes what is surely a crucial task in psychological development. But is it useful to continue to conceptualize that task as *oedipal*? Is understanding of the socialization process enhanced by tying it to a Sophoclean drama of incestuous competition? Is genital rivalry really the fundamental issue that propels a child to transcend the parental orbit?

I don't think that the concept of an Oedipus complex should be discarded altogether, but I do think that Freud's emphasis on it should be reconsidered. Freud conceived of the Oedipus complex as a *universal*, pivotal phase of normal psychosexual development, relevant to the understanding of *every* patient. He thought that in normal development we see resolved oedipal conflict, that unresolved oedipal conflict results in neurosis, and that absence of oedipal conflict indicates failure to "achieve" the oedipal stage of psychosexual development— a sign of severe, early, "pre-oedipal" pathology. Since analysts, like everyone else, tend to find what they're looking for, subscribing to Freud's assumptions concerning the centrality of the Oedipus complex can exert considerable influence on an analyst's clinical work— and not necessarily for the better.

ALICE

Alice came to see me to find out why her love relationships always ended in disappointment: either she stayed too long with an unsuitable man, or she pined hopelessly for someone wonderful who would never become available. Alice's mother had been severely chronically ill, so that as a girl Alice had turned early to her father. He was an extremely accomplished and charismatic man. Alice felt very close to him. Sometimes, when her mother was too ill, Alice would function as his escort or confidante, a role she cherished. At the same time, she resented what she felt were her father's strict demands for her achievement, as well as the fact that he was subject to abrupt rages and withdrawals from her.

Over time, Alice came to experience me in the same way that she had experienced her father. She looked up to me and longed for me. She accused me of being too reserved and concerned with so-called professional boundaries. Ultimately, she brought forward her belief that what she saw as my unnecessary formality represented an effort on my part to protect myself against my attraction to her. She thought this had been the real meaning, too, of the times when her father had been abruptly hypercritical or had withdrawn from her. Just as she had turned to him because of her mother's unavailability, he had turned to her; and the feelings stirred up in him by their closeness had been threatening to him, making him defensive.

Now we could understand Alice's symptoms as caused by the fact that actual childhood events had come too close to a wishful fantasy of oedipal triumph. Alice loved her mother and felt terribly guilty about usurping her mother's place. What she perceived to be her father's misgivings about his intimacy with his daughter only augmented Alice's guilt. Because of that guilt, Alice could not permit herself to share sexual love with a man too much like her father. When she met a man like that, she sabotaged the relationship. She could only seek sexual satisfaction with unsuitable men.

Unfortunately, our formulation of Alice's problem as an inhibition motivated by oedipal guilt, compelling as it was, did not lead to significant change in her life. Her pattern of yearning only for unavailable men persisted. We looked into the possibility that Alice was denying her guilty pleasure at superseding her mother, avoiding acknowledgment of her sadism and her disapproval of it, and a number of related aspects of her oedipal conflict that seemed valid to both Alice and me—all without symptomatic relief.

Alice became concerned that I was growing frustrated—which I was, though I was not aware of expressing my frustration to her. However, what became more and more conspicuous to me about Alice's anxiety was that she imagined my frustration to stem exclusively from my not being able to help her as much as I wished. She never considered that my frustration might include a reaction to any selfish interests of mine being thwarted—my desire to feel effective, my pride in my skill, or my wish to conclude the treatment (I was seeing her at a reduced fee). In Alice's mind, I was motivated entirely by love for her, without a trace of narcissism.

My own view of myself was not quite as noble as Alice's view of me, and the discrepancy directed me to recognize an important idealization that Alice and I had not yet identified and addressed. When I pointed it out to Alice, I was surprised by the extremity of her sudden, abrupt upset. She began to talk for the first time about quitting treatment. Initially, she claimed that she understood me to be implying that I wanted to be rid of her, but eventually she was able to recognize that her idealization of me had protected her against a horror of thinking that I might not be as loving as she believed.

Now her thoughts turned to her father and she became able to admit terribly painful perceptions of him that she had been warding off for many years. With great sadness, Alice acknowledged that her childhood conviction that her father had struggled with his too passionate attachment to her, drawing back when it became dangerously intense, was not really supported by the evidence. Rather, he had been involved with his daughter only when it served his own needs—when he required a hostess, or someone to listen patiently to his self-pitying complaints—and he would drop her completely, without any regard for her feelings, whenever he had no immediate use for her. Then, if she sought his attention she found him coldly unavailable, or irritable and dismissive if he was inconvenienced.

Since Alice had been deprived of her mother by illness, she had depended desperately upon affection from her father. His narcissism and exploitive disregard for Alice was intolerably painful to her—one might say that recognition of it had been incompatible with her psychological survival as a child. Therefore, she had wishfully transformed her experience of her father's neglect into a story of his tortured, secret, incestuous love for his daughter. But beneath what we might call Alice's carefully cherished fantasy of oedipal triumph, there always lay a terrible conviction that she had never been loved and must be unlovable, and it was this conviction that really caused her romantic difficulties. She was sure that she could never be accepted by a man she really loved, and she couldn't bear to repeat her catastrophic childhood experience of rejection.

It was extremely painful for Alice to confront her experience of being unloved, but doing that difficult work also permitted her to realize that she had been living under the burden of a terrible misunderstanding. As she reviewed the events of her childhood, she could see that they did not indicate that there was anything terribly wrong with her—only that she had to contend with very difficult circumstances. It wasn't that she was unlovable; it was that her father had a difficulty in loving. The recognition caused Alice to grieve, but it was also liberating. As a result of the analytic work that ensued, Alice's self-image and what she expected from men began to change. Eventually, she met someone whom she could love who fell in love with her.

Obviously, this was an ultimately successful clinical analysis. Alice got where she needed to go, even though she and I spent a lot of time looking into what was eventually revealed to be a red herring—Alice's "pseudo-Oedipus complex," so to speak. Was this roundabout path necessary? Could my analytic efforts have been more efficient? Would I have helped Alice expose the true nature of her struggles more quickly if I had not assumed the importance of oedipal conflict? It's impossible to say and not terribly important in this instance, given the happy outcome. But in some other instances, misleading assumptions concerning the universality of the Oedipus complex are decisive.

Freud had some wonderfully useful ideas, but he wasn't always right. I think Freud was wrong to consider the Oedipus complex a feature of normal psychological development and to assign it the central place he did in his clinical theory. My own experience has been that the concept of an Oedipus complex—even in its most expanded, contemporary relational version—is useful in understanding some patients, probably not most patients, and certainly not all patients.

18

Desire and Power

It's worth considering for a moment how desire in general, and sexual desire in particular, connect to the crucial matter of *power* in clinical psychoanalysis.

If we read the negotiation literature, we find that the experts in that field tell us that *power within a dyad consists of one person being able to get another to do what the other would not ordinarily do*. Power, thus defined, is obviously relevant to the analytic treatment relationship, since it's an analyst's job to get a patient to do what the patient would not ordinarily do. Departure from the ordinary is required of a patient in order for the patient to participate in an analytic investigation. The patient has to relinquish his or her customary patterns of selective attention and censorship; and departure from the ordinary is required of the patient as well in order for a therapeutic outcome to be achieved, since whatever insight is gained in analysis, the patient must ultimately apply it in the form of new adaptations, often in the face of a considerable sense of risk. Analysts might not like to think of themselves as *getting* their patients to do what their patients ordinarily would not do, because that way of describing an analyst's activity carries connotations of manipulation and suggestion, which analysts hope to avoid. But successful treatment certainly depends upon the analyst's having power of some sort. How is the analyst's power best understood?

Besides the negotiation experts' definition of power, there's Winston Churchill's definition of power, which I've always liked: Churchill defined power as *a set of attitudes and expectations*. This perspective on power directs our attention to the *means* by which one person gets another to alter course; and here we can see the connection between *power* and *desire*, because fundamentally it is by creating an expectation that another's desire will be fulfilled that power over the other is achieved. (This is true even in those instances when one person gains power over another by instilling fear, since it is in the expectation that a desire to avoid harm will be fulfilled that the other does what the other would not otherwise do.)

How does the relationship between desire and power play out in clinical psychoanalysis? It has often been observed that a patient comes to the clinical psychoanalytic encounter desiring to be cured, while an analyst comes desiring to provide a cure; and it's usually assumed that the patient's desire is more urgent than the analyst's, which creates a power gradient with the analyst at the upper end. Furthermore, most theories of analytic technique regard the power gradient as one of the analyst's essential tools—a tool that can be misused, of course, but a sine qua non for successful treatment. Freud conceptualized the analyst's power, based upon the patient's desire, in terms of a necessary "unobjectionable positive transference" to the analyst. The assumption that there is an inherent imbalance of desire within the analytic couple that creates power for the analyst, and that the analyst needs that power in order to do his or her work, has remained prevalent in the field.

We might wonder, though, about the assumption that there is an inherent imbalance of desire within the analytic couple. Doesn't the analyst, as well as the patient, bring strong desires to the clinical encounter? To begin with, there's the analyst's need to make a living; not only to earn his or her daily bread, but to establish and maintain a place in the community—status, a sense of social worthwhileness, and the like. We know the crucial narcissistic value of these things—and their fragility! When appointment times remain open in an analyst's schedule and referrals are few, the analyst may be quite conscious of bringing strong desires to the clinical encounter, desires that a new patient who comes to consult the analyst has the power to fulfill or not to fulfill.

Beyond practical and material desires on an analyst's part, there are the analyst's fundamental motivations for doing clinical work. Many analysts get involved in psychoanalysis, at least in part, out of an effort at self-cure. How often does an analyst's desire to relieve a patient's suffering contain a desire from the analyst's past to have been able to help a loved one in pain? How often does an analyst desire to repair a patient just as the analyst desired, in childhood, to repair someone whose care the analyst needed? How often does an analyst want to help a patient just as the analyst has wanted to be helped? I know that these motivations exist in me and I believe that they do in most analysts. Strong desires, indeed, underlie an analyst's participation in the treatment, and they operate incessantly. After all, an analyst's empathy is based upon the analyst's desires—not ancient desires, mastered and set aside, but current, lively desires. *If we look below the surface, distinctions between the analyst's desire and the patient's desire in the clinical encounter become less absolute.*

As far as desire is concerned, then, analyst and patient meet on ground that is potentially more level than is often depicted. Both analyst and patient bring strong desires to the clinical encounter, desires that are different in some ways—though perhaps different more in superficial appearance than anything else—*but not necessarily unequal desires*. If imbalance of desire within the analytic couple isn't an a priori certainty, then a power gradient in favor of the analyst isn't an inevitable component of the clinical analytic working relationship, either. Rather, a power gradient is something analyst and patient choose to create; and they can, if they wish, choose otherwise.

We might consider that desire and power, like so many other aspects of the clinical encounter, are co-authored by analyst and patient. In other words, if a patient feels more desirous and less powerful than his or her analyst, it is because the patient's attitudes and expectations, to use Churchill's felicitous phrase, have been organized in a particular way. And how does that happen? Of course, the patient brings attitudes and expectations to treatment; but, of course, the analyst does as well.

Regarding an analyst's attitudes and expectations, we have to consider the organizing influence of theory-driven, self-fulfilling prophecies. If an analyst thinks of a patient's desire to be cured as greater than the analyst's own desire to provide a cure, that expectation will be communicated to the patient. A patient may desire to be cured by an idealized analyst; and an analyst may, for any number of reasons, desire to be idealized. Then what can *appear* to be an imbalance of desire within the analytic couple *is actually an interplay of equally strong desires* on the parts of the two participants, but an interplay that is not evident—not evident most importantly because certain of the analyst's desires are concealed. Some well-known, longstanding theoretical principles help institutionalize the concealment. The technical concepts of *analytic anonymity* (see Chapter 6) and *neutrality* (see Chapter 8), for example, presuppose that an analyst can and should achieve a position from which the analyst's personal desires are less involved in the clinical encounter than the patient's; therefore, use of the concepts of analytic anonymity and neutrality encourages both analyst and patient to think of their interaction as proceeding from an inherent imbalance of desire, and to assume that their interaction takes place along a crucial power gradient in favor of the analyst.

Nowhere is the problem of a destructive power gradient in the clinical encounter, established through concealment of the analyst's desire, clearer than in regard to sexuality. Prolonged and arduous exploration of a patient's unrequited romantic interest in his or her analyst was traditionally considered an expectable and essential feature of successful clinical psychoanalysis. It certainly became a popular stereotype; and a critical stereotype, too, inasmuch as the typical picture of a patient enamored of his or her analyst for years on end has often been understood to serve the analyst's financial needs—not to say the analyst's covert personal needs—while yielding little benefit to the patient.

The clinical analytic situation, in which two people meet repeatedly, alone, in private, to discuss the most intimate topics, is inherently seductive. Generation of sexual feelings can hardly be avoided. If one person (the patient) is encouraged to make every effort to acknowledge and express those feelings when they occur, while the other person (the analyst) makes every effort not to communicate them, the illusion of an imbalance of desire is inevitably created and a set of attitudes and expectations established. The analyst, who appears only to be desired, will have power over the patient, who desires.

We can hardly be surprised, then, to note the interesting, if sad, observation concerning so-called boundary violations that when women patients who have been sexually exploited by their male analysts are interviewed, it is quite common for the patient to report that the sexual connection was very important to her *because it gave her a feeling of power within the relationship,* and that it was when the analyst tried to *withdraw* from the sexual connection that she initiated a complaint. In other words, the patient experienced being physically involved with her analyst, which made the desires of *both* parties fully evident, as a *corrective* to what was otherwise an abusive power relationship involving an imbalance of apparent desire! Obviously, in these unfortunate cases the remedy is at least as damaging as the problem that prompted it. But that irony should make clear to us how badly sexual desire and power are often managed in clinical analysis when the analyst participates in a traditionally "appropriate" manner.

SYLVIA

When I was in my mid-thirties, I analyzed a woman of about my own age, Sylvia, whose presenting complaints had to do with her inability to sustain love relationships. She was feisty and playful. I found her quite likable, and I thought she was good-looking. But Sylvia had an edge. She took offense easily, and I could see how being quick on the trigger in what she imagined was self-defense might be getting in her way, romantically. I brought it up when I thought it was happening, especially between us, and that seemed to make a difference.

A bit later, Sylvia began to find reasons to describe her sex life in considerable detail. I got the feeling the main purpose of her descriptions was to have an effect on me. I was looking for a way to speak with her about that possibility when in the middle of a session, while lying on the couch, Sylvia startled me by raising a shapely leg in the air, so that her skirt fell completely away, and adjusting her stocking to a garter belt around her thigh—something in the manner of Marlene Dietrich (whom she resembled, as a matter of fact) in her famous scene from *The Blue Angel*.

I gulped, and asked Sylvia what she was doing. A brilliant question—utterly conventional and pointless—and it got the answer it deserved! "My stocking was slipping," she said archly. Right. We both knew that she wanted to turn me on. And, actually, we both knew more than that. We both knew that she was lonely, she was attracted to me, and I was unavailable. Much of this had not yet been articulated, but it had been implicit in all that we were thinking about and discussing—not to mention in our pleasant rapport, and in the mutual respect and appreciation that was evident in our working relationship. Also, I was aware of how much Sylvia felt she needed to defend herself, and of how, in response to my interpretation of her combativeness, she had let go to a significant extent of her customary style of self-defense.

That was all in my mind in some way when I tried again to address what was happening. I said to Sylvia, "I must be torturing you, because you're sure trying to torture me." "Am I succeeding?" she inquired. "Yes, but I can stand it," I replied. She chuckled, and went on to say, ruefully, that she would like to find a nice young doctor to go out with who would be interested in all her problems. The hour was almost over, and when we ended she surprised me again by turning at the door and saying, "Thank you." I could see that there were tears in her eyes.

It was quite an unusual and touching moment with this ordinarily very self-protective young woman; and it proved to be something of a turning point in our work together. Increasingly, Sylvia became able to tolerate an exploration in depth of her vulnerability, which eventually had a decisive, positive effect on her love life.

For me, this episode was an introduction to the importance of acknowledging that the analyst's desires, every bit as much as the patient's desires, participate constantly in the clinical encounter; and it underlined for me how crucial to effective analytic work it is for the patient, as well as the analyst, to have power within the treatment relationship.

It is by no means simple to know how best to deal with the sexual feelings that can be stimulated in analyst and patient during treatment. If too much attention—or the wrong kind of attention—is paid to them, they can become at the very least disruptive. On the other hand, denial of them sends the message that sexual attraction is too dangerous to be acknowledged and cannot be experienced as a harmless pleasure in the context of a responsible and productive working relationship. The solution to this dilemma has to be an artful compromise, made according to case-specific judgments.

The crucial issue is the analyst's comfort with his or her own sexual feelings. If an analyst is secure that his or her sexual awareness of a patient is natural and appropriately managed, then the analyst will find some way of communicating that to the patient. If an analyst is not in control of his or her sexual feelings, then even the most strenuous efforts to avoid self-disclosure will not prevent the relationship from becoming exploitive—we know that this is the case because, unhappily, there is more evidence for it than we would wish. No principles of technique can be formulated for an analyst to fall back on when dealing with sexual feelings. There are only personal integrity and common sense to rely on. Every analyst will try to communicate helpfully about sexual feelings according to his or her own personal style. Mine, as is evident in the way I responded to Sylvia, tends toward a kind of moderate playfulness. No matter what the analyst's stylistic preference, disclosure of sexual feelings will necessarily be selective.

One summer day, a woman whom I'd been treating for a while came to her session wearing a short dress made of thin, silky material that clung to her body, revealing every curve to advantage. Did my willingness to acknowledge sexual feelings direct me to tell her what was on my mind? Of course not. I could not see that anything useful would be achieved by telling her that I found her attractive; in fact, I could imagine some negative consequences of doing so. I decided to keep my sexual feelings to myself for the same kinds of reasons that would lead me not to express sexual feelings stimulated by, let's say, my teenage daughter or one of her friends. My decision was a matter of common sense, not a choice based on principles of analytic technique.

Now, as it happened, things became more complex when, obviously aware that she had made an impression as she entered my office, the patient asked me coyly, "Like the dress?" I said simply, "You look terrific." She smiled and thanked me. During the session, her thoughts returned a number of times to my appreciation of her as a woman and my apparent comfort in expressing it. That proved to be a useful subject to explore, because my response contrasted with what she had experienced during her teenage years as her father's anxious avoidance of acknowledging her sexual development. I replied to her flirtatious inquiry with a direct, but circumscribed description of my experience of her charms, and it seemed to work out very well. Other ways of handling the situation might have worked out equally well or better. But one thing I'm pretty sure would not have been helpful is if I had stonewalled and avoided confirming a sexual response to her on my part that the patient had already perceived.

19

Significant Others

Many treatments begin by a couple asking to be seen together because they're not getting along and they have different views about why that is. Sometimes, effective consultation to a couple helps them realize that a conflict is being created by their equally reasonable but very different preferences, and that the conflict simply has to be accepted and negotiated with good will. At other times, consultation helps one or the other member of a couple recognize that something he or she is doing creates unnecessary conflict, and recognizing that may lead the person to identify a symptom that is best dealt with in individual treatment.

In the course of a patient's individual treatment, the sequence of events is often the other way around: in the process of exploring his or her distress a patient may reach the conclusion that unreasonable behavior by a significant other is causing problems, and helping the patient assess the validity of his or her conclusion can require knowing the significant other's view of the situation. Also, there are situations in which there is little question that a significant other is getting in the way of a patient's treatment, and the problem becomes how to arrange conditions in which the treatment can proceed—for example, when a spouse's actual mistreatment makes it very difficult for a patient to investigate his or her tendency to imagine being dealt with unfairly.

Under any of these circumstances, it can be useful for an analyst to meet individually with a patient's significant other; or, it can be useful for the analyst to meet with the patient and the significant other together; or, it can be useful for the analyst to send the patient and his or her significant other to someone else for consultation. All three approaches were used in the following treatment.

CHRISTINE

Christine, a woman in her mid-thirties, began treatment in order to overcome inhibitions in her work and in her love life. She was conspicuously attractive and very bright. People had always been drawn to Christine, and she knew that. However, she found herself unable to capitalize thoroughly on her assets. She was extremely successful as a corporate executive, but she seemed unable to progress beyond the middle ranks. Repeatedly, Christine stagnated in positions in which a significant part of the credit for her outstanding work went to her immediate superior. Also, Christine tended to hook up with men less competent than herself, try to help them achieve more, and eventually realize that she lacked respect for them. She often guiltily procrastinated putting an end to a relationship that had long since become unsatisfying.

Since childhood, Christine had learned to be appealing as a survival tactic. She got from surrogates the kind of attention and support she needed, but didn't receive, from her parents. From an early age, she had been welcome in all the neighbors' houses and spent most of her time there. As soon as she could, Christine built an independent life for herself outside her home on the basis of her considerable talent as a golfer. Christine's mother was affectionate but vain, and alternated between being preoccupied with her country-club social life to the point of neglecting Christine, and confiding to Christine inappropriately about her marital problems. Christine's father seemed to pay little attention to her until she began to develop physically, at which time he began to make the fact that he noticed her uncomfortably obvious.

Christine and I looked into any number of aspects of her complex and difficult upbringing in our work together. The most crucial issue seemed to be her conflict over surpassing her older sister, who was apparently less gifted and charismatic than Christine. The two children, left too much to their own devices by their parents, were very close and it pained Christine to see her sister always in trouble, lonely, and lost. She was plagued by the feeling that she ought to wait for her sister to catch up with her. Once Christine realized this, and identified the effect her guilty concern about her sister was having on her approach to career and romance, Christine's inhibitions fell away and she flowered. In time, she founded her own meteorically successful venture capital firm. She met David, an attentive and caring man who seemed to be her equal, and eventually they married. Christine terminated her treatment.

Four years later, Christine called me for a referral for David. She told me that he was having difficulty extricating himself from a corporate situation that had gone sour. David knew he tended to be too much of a nice guy sometimes, and he wanted to change that. I gave Christine a colleague's name, and a short time later she left me a message that David had begun treatment.

A year passed before I heard from Christine again. Now she wanted to consult me for her own reasons. When we met, she described how she had been steadily losing her sexual desire for David over the past several years. Their sex life had declined almost completely, at first due to her disinterest, but then because David, after many rebuffs, stopped trying. They were still good friends and cooperated well to raise their two children, but Christine knew she was contemptuous of David's passivity and that David felt it. It seemed to her that he was hurt and resentful, though they rarely talked directly about what was happening. Christine resumed treatment in order to identify and eliminate whatever she was contributing to the stalemate that was impoverishing their marriage.

Christine wondered whether she was denigrating David by contrasting him with an unrealistic, childishly glamorized image of her father. Alongside her criticisms of her father there had always been an idealization of him that Christine and I had explored at some length in our previous work together. Though an irresponsible narcissist, Christine's father was exciting—and anything but passive. Yet Christine was aware that an invidious comparison of David with her father didn't make sense. David, too, had his romantically attractive side. He had been star quarterback of his college football team. He was smart and very handsome. Christine thought that maybe she felt too guilty to enjoy what she had. Unhappily, neither of these very credible hypotheses helped her become more turned on to her husband.

What did become clear to Christine was her idea that she would be losing something if she "gave in" to David. She was aware of nourishing a grievance toward him, not wanting to let him off the hook. Despite knowing that she herself felt frustrated and deprived, she had a sense that it would be a submission to David to be involved with him sexually. Christine fantasized about calling old boyfriends, although she was aware that she had not actually enjoyed sex with them as much as she had originally with David. She experienced a renaissance of her sexual attraction to me, and imagined how much more competent and assertive a lover I might be than David was.

Christine's attitude of grievance seemed central to her turning off to David. Her feeling was that throughout her childhood she had picked up the slack for her self-centered and inadequate parents, cared for herself in ways that they should have cared for her, and she'd be damned if she would do that again. Christine knew she was taking something out on David that wasn't his fault; but at the same time, she felt that David, too, was letting her down, and she didn't want to have to overlook that. She was angry with David for being too passive in all sorts of ways, including how intimidated he was by her sexual rejections.

David complained to Christine that she ought to be more receptive, while Christine complained to David that he ought to be bolder and more assertive. David felt Christine should be more encouraging, but Christine wanted to see David keep up his end better before she would change her attitude. Obviously, the two had reached a standoff that was held in place by their mutual resentments. Under the circumstances, it was hard for either of them to benefit from individual treatment because each was convinced that the other was the problem. I suggested to Christine that they see a couples therapist to try to adjudicate their differences and unlock the logjam. I suggested that they both needed to be more tolerant and forgiving, but neither wanted to go first. Christine thought couples therapy was a good idea and David agreed. They contacted a couples therapist whom both David's analyst and I respected and arranged a consultation.

It didn't go well. Christine reported to me her impression that the couples therapist seemed to be assigning the major responsibility for the problem to her. Christine could see that the couples therapist suspected her of being overly demanding and rejecting of David because she compared him with her father. This was, of course, an avenue that had been well traveled in Christine's treatment with me. I encouraged Christine to speak frankly in couples therapy about what she didn't like about the therapist's assumptions. She did that, and it seemed to produce a shift. The couples therapist now focused on the reality of David's passivity. Instead of implying that Christine was too exacting, the therapist began to confront David with his lack of assertiveness, telling him that any woman would find it disappointing. This new approach was no better. A cloud of pessimism about the future of the marriage began to descend.

Christine was discouraged and believed that David was, too. She didn't know what direction to take. I suggested that it might be a good idea for me to meet with David to get his view of the situation. After that, the three of us might get together to develop some ideas about how to turn the sexual and emotional decline around. Christine discussed my proposal with David. Both of them were happy to try it.

The chief impression I formed from my meetings with David, who was a very likable and obviously talented man, was that he had inhibitions that he was rationalizing by thinking of them as justifiable responses to Christine's negativity. Christine could, very definitely, be hypercritical and unforgiving. However, it seemed to me that while David's complaints about Christine were reasonable, he was losing sight of the fact that there were ways in which he might, for his own reasons, want to be more assertive with her. I thought that David was avoiding looking into anxieties that were causing him to retreat from Christine, irrespective of his understandable resentment toward her. We had a cordial couple of sessions that David said gave him some things to think about, which he would take up in his own analysis.

Then, in my conjoint meeting with Christine and David, an unexpected thing happened. Christine was complaining about how long it had been since they'd had sex, and David reminded her that several days before (the night following my meeting with him) he'd awakened Christine in the middle of the night and made love to her. Christine admitted that she had no memory of the event, though she had a feeling that it had happened.

When I met again with Christine individually, she puzzled over her amnesia. She had the idea that David had awakened her in the middle of the night and made love to her because he had somehow been emboldened by his contact with me. Christine was aware of feeling uncomfortable about the connection between David's meeting with me and his sexual assertiveness with her, which she thought might have led to her putting it out of her mind. In meetings that followed, Christine reported that David was continuing to be more forward. He had playfully joined her in the bath, which turned her on, but she froze and couldn't take it any further. We focused on Christine's freezing. It was a familiar state to Christine, and thinking about it made her extremely anxious. With great hesitation and difficulty, Christine brought forward a memory of freezing in the same way, feeling panicked and not knowing what to do, when she was a teenager. It was once when her father, slightly tipsy, had kissed her and stuck his tongue in her mouth.

Christine's uncovery of this traumatic memory opened a fruitful avenue of self-investigation for her. She was able to see how being turned off to David had to do with a similarity between the way she felt about him and the way she felt about her father, rather than with a contrast in her feelings about the two of them. Christine was determined to overcome her inhibition and began to have sex with David again. She reported that David had begun to look into his own anxieties in his individual treatment, as he said he would, and that it was helping him be more assertive.

When interviewing with David and Christine as a couple seemed like it might be useful, I first tried to "outsource" the consultation. It seemed possible that some extended work with them might be needed. If that were the case, I didn't think I should be the one to do it because the responsibilities I would undertake toward David and Christine together would likely conflict with my responsibilities to Christine, individually, as her analyst. However, when my referral didn't work out, I realized that it would be very difficult for any couples therapist to become well informed enough to do what needed to be done. It became clearer to me that the primary objective of the consultation was not to treat David and Christine as a couple; it was to gather information, and possibly to intervene for the purpose of facilitating Christine's treatment. Therefore, rather than looking for another couples therapist for David and Christine, I decided to undertake the task myself.

When I'm trying to gain as full as possible a picture of what a patient is dealing with concerning his or her complaints about a relationship, it often seems to me that the most useful thing to do would be to invite the significant other to join us and contribute his or her point of view. But sometimes, the issues involved are such that I suspect that the significant other might feel able to speak more freely— or be able to listen more easily to what I have to say—if I interview him or her alone. Given the nature of the sexual issues between David and Christine, as she described them, I thought that David would probably be more comfortable and open if I saw him by himself.

Traditionally, analysts have avoided meeting with significant others in their patients' lives (a policy that child analysts, of necessity, have had to set aside). One reason analysts have not wanted to meet with patients' significant others is that clinical analysis is traditionally understood to be an investigation into a patient's "internal" reality, not the "external" reality of the patient's life, so that the kind of information that I hoped to gather by meeting with David, then with David and Christine together, is considered irrelevant to psychoanalytic work. I've already discussed why I find the division of reality into "internal" and "external" unhelpful, and how "reality testing" is fundamental to a practical analytic approach (see Chapter 7).

Also, according to traditional theory, if an analyst meets with a patient's significant other, the meeting will be an *enactment* and therefore an interference with psychoanalytic work. There was unquestionably a powerful dimension of enactment in my meetings with David, and my conjoint meetings with David and Christine. Christine and I knew that what transpired definitely corresponded to certain of her fantasies. One of them became explicit immediately: namely, her discomforting belief that my meeting with David permitted me to use him as a proxy to make love to her. Subsequently, Christine and I discussed other meanings that my meetings with David, and with the two of them together, had for her; and there were undoubtedly unconscious meanings that we never discussed. However, since I understand enactment to be a dimension of all analytic events, not something that can or should be avoided (see Chapter 10), I didn't regard the fact that my meeting David would certainly have unconscious meaning for Christine as a contraindication.

20

Stopping

Analytic treatment is brought to a conclusion when sufficient psychotherapeutic benefit has been achieved, or when there is sustained lack of progress toward therapeutic benefit. In either case, clarity and consensus about symptoms and desired symptom relief are required in order to effectively end treatment, just as they are in order to effectively begin treatment (see Chapter 2) and in order to effectively pursue treatment (see Chapter 3). The decision to stop, like any other decision about analytic procedure, is best arrived at collaboratively; but judgments concerning whether adequate symptom relief has been achieved, upon which the decision to stop is based, are ultimately the patient's to make. Ralph's treatment (see Chapter 2) was a very condensed illustration of how this principle applies. I explained to Ralph the options, as I saw them, for how we might proceed. He felt, for the moment at least, that he had gotten what he came for and that he didn't need to meet with me further. We collaborated, in that my input was helpful to him; but he made the decision to stop meeting together, based on his own judgments concerning his symptoms and the symptom relief he had gained even in a short time.

The standard error with regard to ending psychoanalytic treatment is that treatment is not ended soon enough. All too often, an analyst will persuade a patient to stay in a treatment that has not produced therapeutic benefit—or in a treatment that initially afforded some therapeutic benefit but is no longer doing so. Selfish motivations dispose an analyst to hang on too long, rather than to let go too early. Nobody likes to admit failure or to lose a source of income. It's not difficult for an analyst to find rationalizations for recommending that a patient continue in treatment, especially if the analyst considers himself or herself an expert whose understanding trumps the patient's experience of lack of symptom relief. Patients not infrequently get told that they shouldn't "run away" from problematic treatments, that they will profit if they stay and "work it through." However, the truth is that when therapeutic results are not forthcoming, it's usually worthwhile for the patient to try working with someone else. Worst case, the patient discovers that he or she has run into the same problem with a different analyst, which can help clarify for the patient what his or her contribution to the difficulty is. It's impractical to stay in a treatment that isn't resulting in symptom relief. When analytic treatment is proving unsuccessful, the decision to stop is a difficult one to make, and making it well requires the very best in collaboration between patient and analyst.

The same is true when analysis has proved successful, yielding hoped-for therapeutic benefits. The ending of an analytic treatment has traditionally been called *termination*. That is a very unfortunate choice of word. It arises from an idealized misconception of clinical analysis as a comprehensive exploration of a patient's psyche that, when properly done, can be judged complete. Termination denotes finality, whereas, realistically, analyst and patient usually do not know with certainty whether meeting further in the future will be warranted; they can only conclude that treatment has achieved results that seem sufficient unto the day. Christine's treatment (see Chapter 19), which took place in several episodes, illustrates this point very clearly. *Discontinuation,* or some word like it that implies the possibility of resumption at some future date, is a much better term to denote the decision to stop meeting.

When cessation of regularly scheduled sessions is conceptualized as a termination, there is less reason to arrange for follow-up. Presumably, analytic work has been completed. If, on the other hand, treatment is only discontinued, it makes sense to schedule periodic check-in visits; and even if it isn't necessary to meet, an analyst will want to be kept informed about how his or her patient is doing. Discontinuation is provisional; termination is not. There is good reason for an analyst to want his or her patients to know that the analyst cares about what happens to them, and an analyst should want his or her patients to know that the analyst remains available to them as needed. Keeping in touch communicates the analyst's openness to the possibility that the patient may want to do more work at a future point. When treatment is *terminated*, the patient can easily get the idea that the analyst views the work as complete and expects that the patient will have no need to return. Under these circumstances, a patient can be reluctant to contact the analyst for further treatment, worrying that the analyst will be disappointed to discover that a completed analysis has proven inadequate. When a clinical analysis is conceptualized as a thoroughgoing psychic investigation that can be expected to last for many years until it is finally terminated as a completed project, the treatment is much more likely to be experienced as a monumental effort that really ought to be sufficient, once and for all.

When analytic treatment is *discontinued*, with follow-up arranged for and the possibility of further work explicitly acknowledged, it is much easier for analyst and patient to decide to stop meeting, at least for a time. Clinical analyses tend to be much shorter when they are conceptualized as treatments aimed at providing symptom relief, rather than self-explorations in pursuit of insight. It's difficult for an analytic treatment to suffer from being too short; more treatment can always be added, if needed. However, the problem of an overlong analytic treatment is impossible to rectify—the patient can't get his or her wasted time, money, and effort back.

Of course, analysis doesn't necessarily end when analyst and patient stop meeting. Ralph's treatment (see Chapter 2) illustrated this dramatically. In fact, in most treatments there are some lines of self-investigation that a patient only feels free to pursue once the patient knows that he or she will no longer be obliged to talk about them with the analyst. Once in a while, a patient's relationship with his or her analyst actually becomes the major obstacle to achieving further therapeutic benefit—for example, when a subtle state of pathological dependency has been inadvertently established and cannot be resolved. On these rare occasions, it can, ironically, be necessary to discontinue meeting in order for treatment to proceed! A unilateral decision on the analyst's part, over the patient's objections, may be required.

I treated a man whose father had criticized him brutally when he was young. As a result, the patient felt thoroughly inadequate, especially with women. Treatment allowed him to realize how unrealistic his father's criticisms had been. The patient began to feel much more confident and adventurous in his romantic life. But he would always find a way to avoid trying for the women who really attracted him. He dreamt of being an Indian warrior, slaying a wolf and wearing its pelt into battle, where he was invincible. The dream vividly portrayed the patient's experience of our relationship. No matter how much we discussed it, he could not free himself from the belief that he was merely borrowing strength from me, and that if he were too successful, I, like his father, would be displeased and I would punish him by withdrawing the power that I was making available to him.

After a time, when I had tried everything else I could think of without success, I told the patient that I thought our regular sessions were perpetuating his self-underestimation and maintaining his irrational fantasy of dependence on me. He was using me like a fetish, believing that being in my presence enabled him to borrow the strength he imagined me to have, and that was preventing him from realizing how strong he was on his own. Therefore, we needed to stop meeting. He objected, but I insisted and set an ending date a few weeks away. Six months after we discontinued, he called me happily to say that he had found a wonderful woman and that they were moving in together. We met a while later for a few celebratory sessions and agreed that no further work was needed.

Of course, there are patients, often seriously disordered, for whom regular meetings with the analyst continue indefinitely to serve a useful function. For these patients, to discontinue meetings would be a disservice. At the same time, in such cases there is no need to cost the patient unnecessary time and money by pretending that an intensive psychological investigation is under way. Reliable, reassuring contact with the analyst is all that is required; and the purpose can usually be served by a minimal schedule of relatively brief sessions at intervals. Practical psychoanalysis, with any patient, aims to confer maximum therapeutic benefit as efficiently as possible.